VIETNAM dos & don'ts

in Vietnam

By
Claude Potvin & Nicholas Stedman

Illustrations by
Paul Davis

ISBN 974-8279-93-6

Published in Thailand by
Book Promotion and Service Co., Ltd.
2220/31 Ramkhamhaeng 36/1
Huamark, Bangkok 10240
Thailand
Tel: 66 2 7320243-5
Fax: 66 2 3752669
E-mail: publishing@book.co.th

Distributed by
Booknet Co., Ltd.
1173, 1175, 1177, 1179 Srinakharin Road
Suan Luang, Bangkok 10250
Thailand
Tel: 66 2 3223678
Fax: 66 2 7211639
E-mail: booknet@book.co.th

Printed and bound in Thailand by
Amarin Printing & Publishing Public Company Limited

Thank you for buying this book. We welcome your comments. Please send them to
comments@book.co.th

dos & don'ts in VIETNAM

dos
&
don'ts

CONTENTS

page	
1	The Culture
9	Character Traits
19	Vietnamese Way of Thinking
31	Body Language
37	Religion
43	Government & Politics
51	The North & The South
55	Cities & Provinces
61	The Wars
71	Entering the Country
75	On the Road
89	Practicalities
95	Sleeping & Eating
105	The Well-Behaved Traveller
113	Mainly for Men
121	Mainly for Women
127	Shopping
137	Trekking
143	Swimming
147	At a Friend's House
151	Pagodas & Temples
155	Weddings & Funerals
161	Holidays & Festivals
171	Language & Culture
177	Yes or No?
181	Useful Vietnamese Phrases

THE ORIGIN OF THE VIETNAMESE PEOPLE

At a time when the earth was still desolate and uninhabited, a Golden Dragon descended from the clouds circling above the land. As he alighted near the seashore, he transformed himself into a handsome young man. He was Lac Long Quan, ancestor of all the Lac Viet people and father of all the Hung Kings.

Walking along a rocky stream, he encountered a giant tiger holding a white bird in its sharp, curved claws. Lac Long Quan picked up a pointed stone and threw it with all his might at the tiger's breast, forcing it to let go of the bird.

After having killed the beast, Lac Long Quan stood stupefied as the bird suddenly changed into a princess wearing a long, silken gown and a magnificent headdress made of birds' feathers. The princess's name was Au Co.

The two of them erected a stilt house by the bank of the stream and a few years later, Au Co gave birth to a hundred eggs. From these eggs hatched a hundred young boys, already strong and healthy like their father.

In the spring, Au Co and fifty of her sons decided to move up into the mountains, while Lac Long Quan stayed by the seashore with the remaining fifty. Au Co showed her sons how to clear and till the land for agriculture, how to build dykes and irrigation canals to grow rice. Lac Long Quan showed his sons how to fish from the sea and the rivers.

Very soon, villages sprung up in every corner of the land, populous and wealthy. After a thousand years, under the guidance of the Hung Kings, all grandchildren of Lac Long Quan and Au Co, the Viet peoples of the mountains and the deltas carry on their ancestors' mission, building and protecting their land, in times of hardship as in times of peace.

THE CULTURE

Vietnam

Vietnam is Vietnamese

For Westerners travelling through Asia, it is always a surprise to discover countries based largely on homogenous cultures. In many countries throughout the world, development has been associated with population movements and integration, resulting in systems and attitudes reflecting the multicultural nature of its citizens. Vietnam's history is mainly the story of one ethnic group - the Kinh - still representing nowadays 85 percent of the population.

You can integrate in Vietnam as a foreigner... but you will never become Vietnamese if you weren't born Vietnamese. Just look in the mirror if you aren't convinced!

DO remember that Vietnam was specifically fashioned for the Vietnamese, not for foreigners. It's their country and - for the most part - they are extremely proud of it and fiercely nationalistic.

DON'T fall for the stereotype that all Asian countries are alike. Vietnam has its own identity and characteristics, quite different from its neighbours, including China... If you were a Swede, you wouldn't consider yourself the same as a German or even a Norwegian, would you? Similarly, Vietnamese like to think they are unique... because that's what they are!

DO accept that you are a guest in Vietnam and always will be. You will experience what it feels like to be part of a visible minority. Fortunately however, you are part of a rather privileged one.

DO reflect that guests enjoy special status but also have special responsibilities.

DO try to learn as much as you can about the culture, to integrate as much as possible into the life of the people around you, even knowing that you will never become one of them. The Vietnamese will highly appreciate your efforts to understand them, their culture and their language. And you'll benefit from better treatment, better prices and wider smiles.

Culture shock

- Everyone gets it. If you don't, you probably haven't left home yet... physically or psychologically!
- Talk about it, laugh about it, share it with fellow travellers... don't keep it bottled up inside you.
- Don't blame it on the country. If you're looking for home, use your return ticket.
- The cure is at your fingertips: understanding your new surroundings.
- Your responsibility: to learn to enjoy Vietnam for what it is, a country neither better nor worse than home, but incredibly different.

- If this is any consolation in times of utmost despair... Vietnam is host to thousands of expatriates, many of whom don't want to leave. There must be reasons: go out and find them!

DO remember there is no right or wrong in cultural difference: only difference.

Family, the pillar of Vietnamese society

In fact, there are three pillars of Vietnamese society, and they are family, family and family! This could be spelled out as family (immediate), family (extended) and family (projected).

It would be difficult to overestimate the importance of family and the extent to which the 'family' model is present in all of the country's institutions.

Wards and districts are run like extended families. Each government office reproduces the family model with a paternal figure at the helm (usually a man), looking after his 'children' (i.e. employees).

Even in a business environment, employers and colleagues will treat you as

part of an extended family, taking care of you when you are sick, visiting you on weekends and holidays, inviting you to their weddings, funerals, housewarmings, and so on (and expecting to be invited to yours!). Naturally, there is also a downside to all this intimacy: people regularly enquiring about your everyday doings or movements and interfering in your personal life. You'll receive plenty of unsolicited advice - but if you listen, you'll soon learn plenty about how things are done the Vietnamese way!

DO realise that the Vietnamese have a very different perspective on social, political and business organisations, most of which are modelled on the extended family concept.

DON'T be offended if newly made friends poke into every detail of your personal life. They are in fact helping you become part of a Vietnamese group.

DO enquire about your Vietnamese friends' health, families and personal life. It will show interest and respect.

DO understand that family matters are paramount and unexpected family responsibilities will take precedence over appointments and activities scheduled previously.

Take a second look at the legend of the origin of Vietnamese people. All Vietnamese, from the deltas to the mountains, descend from the marriage of a dragon lord (Lac) and an immortal princess (Au Co). The dragon is said to have come south from China and, once all their children were grown up, the dragon and his wife the princess retired to the spirit world. What Vietnamese retain from the story is that all Vietnamese people are related to each other. More than one country, this is one (very) extended family... or at least that's what they would like it to be!

As much as Westerners are 'task-oriented', Vietnamese are 'relationship-oriented'. You have a problem? Work on the relationship.

Ethnic groups

If 85 percent of Vietnamese are of Kinh ethnic origin, that still leaves 15 percent of the population divided among the 53 other ethnic groups.

The most well known of these groups are the Tay, Thai, Hoa, Khmer, Muong, Dao and Hmong, all of whom consist of around a million people each. At the other end of the spectrum are the Co Lao, La Ha and Ngai groups with numbers of less than 2,000, and finally the Pu Peo, Ro-mam and O-du with only a few hundred individuals remaining in each one.

Even if the government is making great efforts to present a positive image of Vietnam's ethnic groups and is trying to ensure their inclusion in the great Vietnamese family, many individuals still consider them backwards and unsophisticated. As in most other parts of the world, ethnic groups and visible minorities have never had it easy. They need all the help they can get.

Without being overly chastising, **DON'T** encourage negative or degrading remarks and attitudes towards ethnic groups.

DO respect cultural differences and whenever possible, choose tour operators who appear more culturally sensitive.

What's a Viet Kieu?

You'll hear this term used very often. It refers to all Vietnamese who have left their homeland to live in another country.

Many are now coming back to Vietnam to conduct business for their own sake or as representatives of foreign companies or organisations. Having someone who understands the local language and customs as well as being familiar with some Western ways is a boon to foreign organisations, but can sometimes also be a mixed blessing.

Most Viet Kieu have left for either political or economic reasons and have not been back for decades. Meanwhile, the country has changed so much it may seem as though they have taken a time machine from the past rather than a plane to come

back to Vietnam. Their ideas, their manners and even their language can seem strange for younger generations. Those who have stayed behind to live through the difficult years will sometimes refer to those who left as deserters or even traitors.

But as more and more Viet Kieu flock back, heeding the call of the government to help in the country's reconstruction efforts, this distrust will vanish and family ties will once more take precedence.

Gender equality

We have no intention of jumping on the gender analysis bandwagon. Numerous evaluations and studies are available to those who would like hard data and detailed interpretation.

Broadly - very broadly - speaking, the Western model of gender equality has few followers in Vietnam, although Vietnamese women are as numerous (if not more) in the business and political arena as they are in most developed countries.

All Vietnamese are proud to mention that their constitution

guarantees equal status to both sexes; however, separate gender roles for men and women, a legacy of Confucian teachings, are still very much ingrained.

The older generations are keen to mention the major part played by Vietnamese women in the nation's history: their key role in the wars, their presence at higher management levels of large state-owned or private enterprises, their important role in family-based businesses, etc.

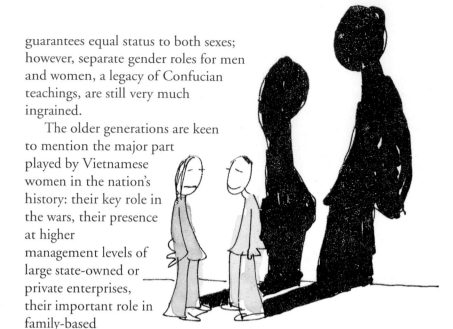

Younger generations, especially the city dwellers, are discovering the challenge of balancing their family ambitions with their professional ones, their traditional Vietnamese ideas on feminism with the trendier worldwide ones.

DO discuss with old and young alike to discover their attitudes and perceptions on gender roles. Most Vietnamese love to discuss this subject... seriously or jokingly... but they will resent condescending or 'colonialist' attitudes.

DON'T judge what you cannot yet understand. As always, respect is the key word here.

CHARACTER TRAITS

Vietnam

Respect

This is an important aspect of Vietnamese society: respect of age, of profession, of wealth... It is important that you show respect in general, as it will usually be shown to you by most Vietnamese in most situations.

DO be reassured that, as a foreigner, you can get away with just about anything - so long as you do it with politeness and respect ... (A Vietnamese friend of the authors puts it this way: "You see, we know foreigners are different, so we forgive them a lot...")

DON'T be afraid of 'doing the wrong thing' or inadvertently insulting or upsetting people in Vietnam: it's a lot harder to do than you'd think! Many people who travel to Vietnam believe they will give terrible offence if they forget to remove their shoes on entering someone's house, or point at someone with their index finger. In fact, the Vietnamese are very tolerant of the foreigner's lack of knowledge of local customs and most transgressions will be seen as minor. For important matters, don't worry: you will be gently and firmly guided along the proper path. Or you'll be dead before you hit the ground... (Only kidding!)

A Westerner went to visit a sick colleague in hospital. En route he stopped to buy flowers and then to pick up several Vietnamese colleagues. "- But he's not dead yet!" said one of them, seeing the flowers the Westerner had bought. The crestfallen fellow hastily asked the driver to turn back to allow him to exchange the 'funeral' flowers for a more suitable bouquet. "Don't worry", intervened his Vietnamese colleagues, smiling: "you're a Westerner!"

As in many Asian countries, an important thing to remember is, if at all possible,

DON'T lose your temper. This is usually seen as a lack of respect for others (who are in their own country, after all) and, what is worse, a lack of respect for yourself: to lose your temper is to lose face, and in Vietnam, not losing face is what it's all about.

DON'T accept this last rule of thumb as a golden one, however: if, after lengthy negotiations, cajoling, smiling, counting to ten while breathing through your nose, nothing has happened, you can always try losing your temper as a last resort. The Vietnamese do it sometimes, so it must work occasionally. Even if it doesn't, you'll probably feel a whole lot better. The key thing is **DON'T** be aggressive if no-one is being aggressive to you: naked aggression is not admired as a quality of leadership or of anything else in this country and bullies get short shrift (see our section on The Wars).

Politeness

Although in many ways a very polite and courteous lot, you may sometimes find people in Vietnam to be quite rude by your own standards.

DO remember that a lot of behaviour in Vietnam is dictated by an incredible density of population. About 80 million souls are for the most part squeezed into the low lying areas around the two big fertile river deltas (the Red River in the north, the mighty Mekong in the south) and along the very narrow coastal plain that links the two together. Which means that if you want to get anything done in this life, you may well have to put your elbow into your neighbour's ribs to get past him. Please remember to do it gently, and with a nice smile on your face. So, **DON'T** bother with queuing up for things: queues and line-ups just don't happen in Vietnam. You just go for it, as though the gaggle of people in front of you were a mirage caused by the sun, waving your money,

tickets, paperwork or whatever in the air and calling out imperiously to be served next. Everyone does it, so instead of fuming at the back of the pack, you'd better start doing this as soon as you arrive (and that includes the airport).

Also, **DON'T** be offended by personal questions and remarks: people will often ask not only surprisingly nosy questions like: "how old are you?", "where are you going?", "why are you late?" but also make quite wounding personal remarks, such as: "why are you so fat?" and "your husband is quite ugly!" These would obviously be considered very rude in many cultures - but not this one.

Humour

Humour can be a valuable tool in Vietnam. The Vietnamese truly love to have a laugh about almost anything - and someone who can crack a joke will be appreciated, find it easier to fit in and, bizarrely, may even be taken more seriously by colleagues or associates - and indeed by any local.

The monosyllabic, tonal nature of the Vietnamese language also makes puns and plays on words particularly popular. You'll be making a lot of these without even realising you're doing it when you speak some Vietnamese: that's why people will often fall about laughing when you say anything, however simple or banal you thought it was!

DO joke about things as a polite way of dodging the many questions you may not want to answer ("Can I come and visit you tomorrow morning before breakfast?", "How much did you pay for that?") or as a clever way to defuse almost any kind of difficult situation. If you manage to have a laugh with people when you bargain, you'll get a better deal when the time comes to fix a price. And you can gain people's trust or sympathy much more easily than by any other means.

HAPPY   SAD   ANGRY

DO realise that Vietnamese people also laugh when they are sad, angry, embarrassed, puzzled, uneasy, shy, grieving, etc. - so laughter (literally) covers a lot of situations!

All sounds too good to be true?

DON'T forget if you get stopped by the police with five kilos of heroin in your backpack, try slipping on a false nose and doing a funny walk. The firing squad will probably still shoot you, but they may have a laugh when they do it.

Political correctness

Forget about political correctness, or at least in the Western sense of the term. In Vietnam, a blind person is blind; a dwarf is a dwarf. Even more so, an ugly person is plug-ugly and a fat one is simply fat. You don't have to mince your words, because the Vietnamese won't. Not when they are with you, nor when they are among themselves. But, believe it or not, it's all done with respect and, more often than not, with a smile. 'How fat you are!' they will say while patting your belly or assessing the size of your

arms. You'll get your body hair pulled and your bald head stroked. They'll point and laugh... and the best response is to laugh with them. If you can't accept yourself as you are, Vietnam might not be a wise choice of travel destination for you.

The politically correct Vietnamese is a different breed. While he might say his boss is afraid of his wife or has short ears (long ears are considered the lucky and beautiful ones), he would not comment on his superior's capacities to run the office or on his role as a leader. Bitching about your boss, the society, your country, your leaders is definitely NOT politically correct in Vietnam. Leaders command respect, like parents in a family. If you disagree with them, you try and keep that rather private.

Of course, there are exceptions. You will find rather significant differences in their voicing of political opinions between Northerners and many Southerners. Read your history books to understand the different perspectives. But remember, it's one thing for Vietnamese to criticise their system; it's another to hear foreigners do it. In Vietnam as

in any other society, unless you are very familiar with the local context, tread softly on political and religious matters.

Shyness and smiles

Younger people, particularly women, often appear painfully shy to foreign eyes.

DO understand, however, that to a great extent this is the

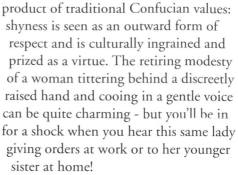

product of traditional Confucian values: shyness is seen as an outward form of respect and is culturally ingrained and prized as a virtue. The retiring modesty of a woman tittering behind a discreetly raised hand and cooing in a gentle voice can be quite charming - but you'll be in for a shock when you hear this same lady giving orders at work or to her younger sister at home!

Smiles are more complicated: it's a very Vietnamese trait, and people will smile at you wherever you go. This aspect of Vietnam maybe makes for a much more agreeable initial contact with people than in, say, Poland (sorry Poland!); but **DO** be aware that the Vietnamese smile in many situations where Westerners - and even most Chinese or other Asians - would certainly not.

One of the authors of this book still remembers an early bicycling encounter with Vietnamese traffic that included a near-death experience. Narrowly escaping the crushing wheels of a truck and briefly coming almost face-to-face with its unconcerned driver, he reacted in a totally non-Oriental way, screaming invective in any language that came to mind. According to the local order of things, the responsibility for avoiding any collision was entirely the cyclist's; no apology could be expected, nor was given. The only reaction from the driver was a fixed, humourless, toothy smile. Not a commiserating smile, not a derisive smile: simply an instinctive reaction to an alien and embarrassing situation, provoked by a (possibly insane?) foreigner.

More generally, emotions are expressed very differently by Asian peoples, when they are expressed at all. For instance, in

Vietnam, embarrassment is mostly accompanied by smiles and overall sympathetic facial gestures. This is in sharp contrast to the Western way of showing embarrassment with downcast eyes, lowering of the head and a serious face. Misinterpretation is but a smile away. All this can take some getting used to for the newcomer: even when you are aware of it and have assimilated this intellectually.

However baffling or mysterious Vietnamese smiles sometimes are, they can also often be a very uplifting experience. If you are travelling through the countryside late in the day as the sun begins to set, when workers walk or cycle home from the fields, elated by the end of long hours of hard labour, your path will be lined with smiling, waving adults and children. It makes you feel awfully important: a bit like royalty, acknowledging the acclaim of your loyal subjects. It also can make your smile muscles and waving arm quite exhausted!

There is however an exception even to the ever-smiling reputation of the Vietnamese. Smiles are definitely NOT part of the Government clerks' uniform. If you can wrench one from the bank teller, the post office lady or the train ticket salesperson, count yourself lucky.

Stubbornness

Look at history!

Being stubborn is perhaps perceived as more of a virtue than a vice in Vietnam: people were stubborn with the Americans 30 years ago, with the French 50 years ago, with the Chinese goodness knows how many times over the last 1,000 years. The Vietnamese are rightly proud of their unparalleled record of resistance to foreign domination, and naturally remain rather sensitive on this point: as a foreigner, giving orders to a local can require some cultural sensitivity - particularly if you actually want them to do as you say!

DO be advised that a Vietnamese will only very rarely show disagreement by confrontational means or even with a straight "no". Nine times out of ten, he/she will say "yes", along with one of those lovely smiles we were just discussing, and then just not do it: it's as simple as that.

DO learn from the experts: when you're bursting to say "no way, pal!", bite your tongue, smile and say "ye-e-s". Culturally, it's rarely a good move to say "no" right off the bat. Your opening gambit is "yes", leaving you plenty of time to make up some excuse, forget all about it, or simply do the opposite.

VIETNAMESE WAY
OF THINKING

Good and bad tempers

It tends to be the accepted wisdom that Vietnamese people never really lose their tempers or get angry in public. Such behaviour is certainly rarely admired and is generally seen as unbecoming, or even degrading, rather than assertive. However, like most nuggets of accepted wisdom, all this is quite true - but only up to a point. If you go beyond that point, well... you may see someone snap and lose it - big time! When repressed irritation and anger finally escape, they generally do so under high pressure.

So it's not impossible you'll witness people seeing red after a minor road accident, or something similar. But does this mean that you, too, can throw a fit if you think the situation calls for it? Well, maybe not...

DO remember that, however exasperating a situation may become,

1) You may not have all the necessary elements in hand to understand fully what is going on.

2) Part of the problem is going to be your own lack of local language skills (not everyone speaks English as well as you do!).

3) It really isn't a good idea for you to go wading in aggressively like a bull in a china shop (or like a G.I. on China Beach...). At 80 million Vietnamese against one (that's 01) of you, the odds will never look good.

4) If you lose it, you're as good as accepting that, basically, you've lost. You may feel better in the short term, but you're very unlikely to get results after that outburst.

5) When you really have to tear someone off a strip, take care not to do it in front of others: always leave space for saving face.

6) Discretion is almost always the better part of valour: smile, even if it physically hurts sometimes. This way, you'll live to fight another day...

DON'T give up, though: keep asking leading questions in order to verify and extend your knowledge of the situation. Information is rarely volunteered spontaneously, but if you find the right question, you may get a straight answer (see our section entitled Yes or No? starting page 177).

Industrious, but fate dictates all

It's easy to conclude that the Vietnamese are an industrious people and that theirs is a country on the move: everywhere you look there are people bustling and hustling. Bustling that you'll see includes repairing roads, building houses, working the land or fishing the sea. Hustling covers all the markets, shops, bars, cafés, restaurants, soup joints, street sellers, taxis, motorbike taxis, pedicabs, shoeshiners and so on who will line your path wherever you (and everyone else) goes.

DON'T assume, however, that all locals have a work ethic identical to that valued in many Western cultures: they don't. True, many actually hold down two or even more jobs at the same time and people are quite capable of driving themselves into the ground for their own advancement, or for that of their families (which amounts to the same thing in this culture). But being employed by anyone else is a slightly different kettle of fish.

Let's begin with working for the (still huge) state sector, which is perhaps an extreme case in point.

DO consider, when you're buying a train ticket, posting a parcel or booking into a state-run hotel, that these kinds of jobs are no longer viewed as quite the prestigious positions they once were, as salaries are worth less and less and guaranteed lifetime job security is fast being eroded. Service may sometimes reflect this.

The vast majority of teachers are also employed by the state - for their official job, at least. There is a popular joke in Vietnam that goes, Teachers say: "The Government pretends to pay us; we pretend to teach; and the students pretend to learn..."

These public bodies are also organised in a very hierarchical manner (in fact, a very patriarchal manner, as we mentioned earlier). This means that only a very select minority is used to making decisions and to being responsible or accountable in their work. At the risk of generalising, most of the rest tend to do only the strict minimum, and only when they are told to do it. Unfortunately, it must be said that this often holds true for people now employed in well paid and prestigious positions. This attitude of 'doing as little as you can get away with' can be very frustrating for Westerners trying to work or do business in Vietnam.

We have heard of a recent example to illustrate this last point, concerning half a dozen translators and secretaries employed by a major joint venture medical facility. These employees, extremely well paid by local standards, began to arrive at work exhausted, many being found fast asleep in their offices during working hours. It emerged that, in accordance with local custom, they had all found extra jobs to bring even more money home for themselves and their families. They were coming to work to get some rest in their air-conditioned offices! Of course, you could argue that this is a work ethic of a kind...

Let's move on to the *but fate dictates all* bit of this section. Now then, we just mentioned that being responsible and accountable are not among the most obvious Vietnamese virtues. In fact, some foreigners who have been here for a while like to remark dryly that the word 'accountability' is untranslatable into the local lingo. Not strictly true, but they do have a point.

Some of this can be explained by the undeniable fact that the Vietnamese are a truly fatalistic people, and if no-one else can be blamed for their shortcomings or wrongdoings, then everything is laid firmly at Fate's door. If something bad or even just negative happens, well, it was going to happen anyway, because it was all written up beforehand in Destiny's Celestial 10,000-Year Planner, and there ain't nothing any puny human being could do to change it one jot...

This can lead to behaviour that may be difficult to understand for outsiders. For example, a man who is injured in some way will attract a curious crowd, but will often receive no first aid or even assistance from any of the onlookers, even if he's bleeding to death or his heart has stopped beating. Why? Well because, according to

traditional beliefs, if Fate alone decrees whether he is to live or die, then there's no point wasting energy in doing anything to help him. But another reason offered by Vietnamese friends - a bit paradoxical, this one - is that people are afraid of getting involved and then being held responsible if the injured party dies or similar. "Vietnam: the land that logic forgot", as a friend of the authors puts it (rather uncharitably...).

Such a fatalistic mind-set may also help to explain the popularity of one of the rare manifestations of true lawlessness you just might see while you are in Vietnam: road-racing. Young men on souped-up scooters - often with the brakes taken off and the girlfriend put on the back - drive hell-for-leather through the streets of a town, or even from one town to another. While this can be done for a bet, it is also simply a source of youthful excitement (in itself a rare commodity for the tens of millions of young people in Vietnam). Such races are extremely dangerous on roads where it is almost impossible to drive rapidly in safety and many people - participants and passers-by - are killed or injured. To spice things up a little, the girlfriend riding pillion will sometimes put her hands over the driver's eyes for a few moments. Once again, it is Fate, not dangerous driving, that will decide if they live or die.

DO place your faith in the stars when in Vietnam: horoscopes also play an important part in this deterministic vision of the world. For example, many marriageable young men and women are ruled out from the word go as potential mates because they were born under an incompatible sign of the Vietnamese (same as the Chinese) horoscope. Another example: when the French football team couldn't score a single goal at the 2002 World Cup Finals, nobody was to surprised in (football-crazy) Vietnam: it was common knowledge that their coach was having a terrible horoscope year for achieving anything in that line of work.

DON'T worry, though, because there are no rules against you (or your parents) giving your destiny a helping hand: on auspicious days to be born, hospitals are often choked with pregnant women demanding to have their labour artificially induced or even asking to give birth immediately by Caesarean section. However, these practices are not seen as quite so auspicious by modern medicine.

There's also a Vietnamese version of a *Feng Shui* expert to be consulted on how to position your new house and when to start building it. And you can forget about moving into rented accommodation on the first of the month: a squint at a lunar calendar will almost certainly be a necessary first step to your landlord (not you!) choosing an auspicious day for that activity and for others.

And so it goes on: such beliefs and superstitions are strongly adhered to in Vietnam and add much to the richness and exoticism of its culture.

Tolerance and patience

The Vietnamese are very tolerant of:
- Bad driving
- Noise
- Interruptions
- Invasion (or absence of) personal space
- Discomfort (primitive living and working conditions, being squeezed into a crowded bus for hours on end)
- Sharing everything (food, clothes, books, computers, exam answers, combs, beds, germs, - literally everything)

The Vietnamese are not very tolerant of:
- Insubordination (authority, be it familial, professional or official, should at the very least be seen to be respected)
- Criticism of Vietnamese culture
- Difference displayed by their own people (foreigners actually benefit from a much greater tolerance!). For instance, things can be difficult for women who choose not to marry or have children, for people who lead unconventional lives, who utter unconventional opinions or even who have an unconventional appearance. From a Western perspective, life in Vietnam, including what you might think of as your private existence, is mostly lived according to a series of fairly rigid social norms. Homosexuality, for example, though obviously present, is still largely taboo in Vietnam.

We now have just a few things to say about patience, if you don't mind waiting a few minutes. Despite certain hidden strengths, the Vietnamese would probably not win patience medals at the ASEAN Games.

DON'T miss the spectacle of motorcyclists at a closed railway crossing: people squeeze through as the gates are being pulled across the road and the train is bearing down on them, whistling wildly. Then the rest spread out across the whole width of the road and, as the gates are reopened, try to fight their way through the identical crowd doing the same from the other side...

However, there are situations where people seem incredibly patient to Western eyes. Examples that spring to mind include wrestling with bureaucracy, closing any sort of deal, and when the first auspicious day to get married or to start building a house is not before next summer or even next year. Still more extreme, if you're unlucky enough to lose one of your parents while you're engaged, you and your sweetheart should wait three years before tying the knot. Incredibly, many people do. Now there's patience for you!

Truth and lies

We should maybe begin this section by stating the obvious: Vietnam is not a Judeo-Christian society. Which means, among other things, that lying is not really seen as a sin. It is, as often as not, fine to lie your head off. This does not mean that the country is crawling with malicious fibbers, but rather that truth may be yet another relative concept from that prevalent in your own culture.

The most important thing in a Vietnamese context is to say the right thing (i.e. what should be said in that situation), or, crucially, NOT to say the wrong thing. People will often tell you what they think you want to hear. This is intended to make life more agreeable for you, but it may take you some time to adjust to it (about ten years should do the trick).

DON'T feel insulted if a Vietnamese person smilingly tells you what you know to be barefaced lies: try to remember that that is just how things are here - between locals as well.

DO be wary of any important or controversial information you haven't checked with an independent source: ask, confirm, reconfirm, crosscheck, ponder, then try to make your own synthesis. Vietnam is a country that requires a high tolerance to ambiguity.

Nosy and curious

Are the Vietnamese nosy and curious? The answer, as you'll soon find out for yourself, is an emphatic 'yes!' - But then, you'd be eager for information from the outside world if your country had been kept tightly shut for almost 20 years, wouldn't you?

The truth of the matter is, people in Vietnam are much, much more gregarious and happier to share intimate space with others than we in developed countries have become in our comfortable, compartmentalised lives. This makes people sometimes seem by comparison extremely indiscreet and intrusive. If it's any consolation, they're only slightly more intrigued by a crazy foreigner than by their next-door neighbour. However, if you happen to be a dull, uncharismatic bore, then here's your chance of a lifetime to become a star! Some people clearly miss the attention when they leave Vietnam...

There are a series of questions that you will be asked time and time again by Vietnamese people when you meet them for the first time.

DON'T be offended and try not to be exasperated by these -

often rather personal - repeatedly asked questions. The questioner is at the same time showing a polite interest in you and also executing a central cultural and linguistic ritual that needs a little background explanation.

Briefly, when a Vietnamese person meets a stranger, be they foreigner or fellow countryman, she or he (and it makes a difference) has to choose between 27 (or thereabouts) personal pronouns just to be able to say 'you' and 'I' in Vietnamese. What she is doing, in fact, is projecting the stranger as a theoretical new member into her family to see where he would fit into that hierarchy. To do this, she needs to know at least his age and family situation. She obviously doesn't need to know this just to speak to him in English, but cultural habits die hard - and she's got to talk to him about something...

Here are the usual opening gambits with some suggested answers in brackets:

Where are you from? (Any easily recognisable country will do)

Where are you going? (Don't bother getting too philosophical with this one: it is actually a literal translation of a Vietnamese greeting that would be better rendered as, "Hi, how are you doing?", or similar)

How old are you? (Well, how old are you? - Oh and remember, in Vietnam, you start counting nine months further back with your conception, and everybody adds on a year at *Tết*, the Vietnamese new year, - so how much does all that make?)

Are you married? (Usually prudent to say "yes", unless of course you're looking for action or to settle down in Vietnam and run a noodle stall for the next 20 years)

Do you have any children? (The correct answer is "yes", particularly if you're a woman and a day over 25, but you can fall back on 'not yet' as a stopgap)

How much did you pay for that? (Too much, probably, if you bought it in Vietnam; but you could always try "Shhh! It's a secret..." or "I'm sorry, I can't say: my wife/husband would kill me if I told you!")

How much money do you make a month? ("It depends", "not enough" or "I've forgotten" are to be preferred over "fifty grand" or similar: why bother bragging emptily to people who, if they are asking you the question, are almost certainly earning a fraction of what you get - and forget about trying to explain your higher cost of living, etc.: if you have money - and since you're a foreigner who has travelled to Vietnam, you obviously do - then you can pay more, according to local logic).

Just to finish, a few classic examples of things to watch out for on the 'nosy' front if you entertain at home:

• If you invite people to your house and leave papers or photos visible, they may well be inspected and passed around. This is not considered rude.

• If you invited these people round for a meal, they'll probably nip into the kitchen to have a peek under the saucepan lids to see what strange fare you're concocting for them. (Don't forget to do the same thing to them - if they ever invite you back).

• If your wife is still wandering about upstairs looking for a bra, then tell your guests, as clearly as you can, not to go off exploring, or she may get quite a shock if she bumps into an intrigued advance party.

A French friend recounted the following anecdote after her first trip back to France with her new Vietnamese husband.

While they were staying on a big campsite, her husband, a keen player of card games, noticed a group or family of long-stay campers having a game under their caravan awning. Much as he would have done in Vietnam, he sauntered over to watch the game, unwittingly crossing the (probably) invisible dividing line that marked what these Westerners saw as their inviolable camping territory. The campers looked so aghast and then hostile that the poor fellow left without having seen a single card played...

Punctuality

Generally, people are very dependable when they are required to turn up and put in an appearance at a certain time. The only snag is that they might well arrive too early: **DO** take this into account if it is not convenient, and compensate accordingly.

Deadlines, however, are a different matter: they're rarely, if ever, respected. Everything takes more time than what people first told you. A popular notion that may or may not save you when things get tight is 'thời gian cao su', or 'rubber time'...

One of the reasons for this failure to meet deadlines is simply that the Vietnamese are relationship-oriented, not job-oriented, perhaps giving them a natural advantage as public relations people, but not as planners. A reactive mentality prevails, probably a legacy of war, poverty and natural disasters, evoking a hand-to-mouth existence of precarious subsistence with an uncertain future ahead. But like many things in Vietnam, this is changing.

BODY LANGUAGE

Vietnam

Handshake not wai

You'll likely see more foreigners using the *wai* (the Thai traditional greeting where the palms are clasped in front of the body) than Vietnamese! Either they're arriving from neighbouring Thailand or have read the wrong guidebooks. What's even funnier is when you see the Vietnamese *wai-ing* back out of politeness, imitating the foreigners who are themselves thinking they are conforming to local custom.

Wai-ing is simply not Vietnamese. True, in days of old, Vietnamese used the Chinese hand-over-closed-fist gesture, but the only place you'll still see this is in Chinese films depicting the long gone days of Emperors and mandarin courts.

Having said that, the Thai *wai* will be found in the following limited circumstances:

a) In a Buddhist religious context when praying at the pagoda or greetings monks.

b) In several ethnic minority communities more closely linked to Thai or Khmer groups.

c) In a somewhat transformed gesture when VIPs or guests are applauded by a crowd.

Everywhere else, it's either a handshake or a simple nod of the head. The rule is quite straightforward:

a) With Vietnamese men, you always use a handshake, be you male or female.

b) With Vietnamese women, you wait for them to initiate either a handshake (this is the more modern way of greeting) or you acknowledge their head nod with the same (this is the more traditional way). In case of doubt, opt for the head nod; you won't embarrass anyone with that.

However formal or cold a handshake (or the absence of one) might seem, you'll find the Vietnamese to be quite physical in their contacts even among strangers or with foreigners. But remember: this is between men or between women... not between the sexes. A warm greeting can start with an interminable handshake, followed by a hug of the shoulders and a bout of hand holding that can last the whole discussion. Hands on thighs when men sit discussing, or arms over shoulders for women are also common.

You'll see soldiers holding hands - or sometimes just two fingers - in the street. Your interpreter, on her first visit to a village, might end up taking her siesta curled up to a first-time acquaintance. None of these gestures have any sexual overtones. But, especially for Western men, it does take a bit of getting used to.

Gestures to avoid

Unless you're at a decidedly Buddhist religious site, or with minorities coming from Khmer or Thai descent, you can pretty well forget all the old clichés about 'not touching the head' or 'not pointing with your feet' (hey, do you really point with your feet back home?).

In fact, there are very few gestures that can cause you or your Vietnamese friends real embarrassment.

DON'T employ the Western way of signalling someone to come, by wiggling an upward-pointing index finger. Get used to the Asian way, which is the wiggling of all four fingers together, palm facing down.

DON'T use the Western sign for good luck, with the second finger curled over the index. This has a totally different meaning here, as it refers to the female sexual organs. It is considered a very rude and bad mannered gesture. As is the (rather obvious) inserting of the index finger in a circle formed by the thumb and index finger of the other hand.

DO relax... apart from the previous gestures, unless you're obviously and desperately trying to insult people, you won't get into any serious trouble.

Public displays of affection

As in the rest of Asia, public displays of affection are not encouraged. Although you will see the younger generations trying to pick up Western ways, kissing and hugging in public is still considered impolite and disrespectful. Avoid it, if at all possible.

Even more important is to avoid any physical contact or display of affection towards Vietnamese colleagues of the opposite sex. You risk embarrassing them terribly and having them lose face and reputation in front of friends and colleagues.

But times are changing and many young people are adopting more open manners, especially towards foreigners. For instance, young women will occasionally take the arm of a foreigner for a picture, will give him a big hug on departure or will drop a casual arm on a shoulder.

DO let them initiate such actions and model your own behaviour to their level of comfort.

Cleanliness and smartness

Vietnamese attach considerable importance to their appearance and cleanliness. Very few people - however poor - let themselves be seen in dirty clothes and with tangled or matted hair. Even construction workers, who literally live on building sites, shower every day and wash their - albeit very old - clothes.

However, some notions of cleanliness and personal hygiene are relative: you may observe such common scenes as modish young women waiting at traffic lights busily excavating unwanted waste matter from their delicate nostrils, or hormonal young men intent on bursting blackheads with the aid of a motorbike mirror... Of course, the positive side to this is that it leaves you pretty free to do the same, should the spirit move you. Note also that Vietnamese society is relatively tolerant of the unshaven look, possibly more so than of fully grown Western beards, in fact: it is usually only elderly men here who sport Ho Chi Minh-style wispy outcrops that trail from patriarchal chins.

Vietnamese find nothing cool (yet!) about torn jeans, oversized loose shirts or antiquated and world-savvy T-shirts. They just can't understand how someone who has enough money to travel to foreign countries can be so lacking in self respect as to dress scruffily. They have developed two expressions to designate backpackers: *tây ba lô* and *tây bụi* (meaning 'Westerner with a packsack' or 'dirty - literally dust - Westerner'). Try to stay in the first kind if you want to earn any respect from the local population.

THE BACKPACKER

RELIGION

A bit of context...

Vietnam's traditional religious background is based on three great philosophies and religions - Confucianism, Taoism and Buddhism - that coexist with a more ancient but still thriving Mother worship cult, ancestor worship, popular beliefs, superstitions and ancient Vietnamese animism. It is a rich and finely balanced amalgam that permeates not only the spiritual side of Vietnamese life (most will say they are Buddhists) and their understanding of the universe (taken from Taoist philosophy), but also regulates family and civic duties (which is the main focus of Confucianism).

For number crunchers

Although religious identification is not such a clear-cut matter, statistics tell us that about 70 percent of the population are Buddhist, 10 percent Catholic, 3 percent Cao Daist, 2 percent Hoa Hao and the rest of various other religious groups such as Protestantism, Islam, Hinduism and the specific beliefs of some ethnic minority groups.

Religion and politics

Is religion a sensitive issue in Vietnam? To understand the 'yes and no' answer, one must remember that, from the dawn of civilisation, religion has gone hand in hand with politics, power and conquests.

As far as individual beliefs are concerned - especially those of foreigners - Vietnam has to be one of the most tolerant societies. Actually most Vietnamese couldn't care less if you believe or what you believe in and will not try to convert you to their own sets of beliefs. Winning converts doesn't seem to be a Vietnamese trait although some Western religions did their best to change that state of mind.

However, it is also true that some religious groups are under closer scrutiny than others. Not for their underlying philosophies and values, but for their perceived intervention in the political arena. The role of their followers during the struggle against colonialism and during the American War has influenced the level of control placed on many groups. For instance, in the 1930s, Cao Daism was turned into a political force to fight the French occupation, while most Catholics remained more supportive of the Western presence.

In a still nervous 'post-civil war' environment, the Government is also extremely wary of 'hostile forces' trying to infiltrate Vietnam or raise followers abroad. Many of those anti-Government groups have apparently used religious covers to camouflage their actions. Recently, in 2002, incidents at the Cambodian border have again rekindled this fear of 'hostile forces' disguised as missionaries.

DON'T be afraid to talk philosophy and religion with your Vietnamese friends and acquaintances. Most will be extremely happy to take you to their pagodas and explain their rituals.

DON'T engage in any missionary or conversion activities. This could lead to serious consequences. If this is your mission in life, you might want to consider other countries. What Vietnam needs now is a generation of peace and stability, not more foreign power influences. Any compassionate God will agree to wait a generation...

DO visit all the temples, pagodas and churches you want, ask all the questions you please; just remember to respect other beliefs as you would like yours to be respected.

See page 151, Pagodas and Temples, for additional tips.

Temple or pagoda?

Not that it probably makes much difference to the Gods themselves, but many visitors seem fascinated by this semantic question: what is the difference between a temple and a pagoda?

In English, 'temple' is a more general term designating any building where people go to worship, while 'pagoda' more specifically refers to a Hindu or Buddhist temple.

Vietnamese also uses two main words *đền* and *chùa* translated respectively as 'temple' and 'pagoda'. *Chùa* refers to temples dedicated to the worship of Buddha. *Chùa* are tended by resident monks (those shaven-headed, saffron-robed guys). On the other hand, *đền* are temples where all other deities are worshipped. They are tended by ordinary men or women assigned to each temple. Some pagodas - especially in the North - will comprise, in addition to the most important altar to Buddha himself, other altars to different deities. Thus, using the Vietnamese definitions of the words, one can find temples *(đền)* inside pagodas *(chùa)*.

In the Vietnamese spiritual world, many deities are actually real human beings that have lived exceptional lives and have kept their influential position in the afterlife. Buddha is the highest ranking of all. Others deities of human origin include famous and powerful emperors, mandarins and national heroes that influenced Vietnamese history. Buddha the compassionate has to take care of everybody, irrespective of his or her deeds and situation. He is therefore extremely busy and does not have time to cater to each individual prayer. However, other figures are choosier, they will look upon individual prayers and decide which one they will answer favourably. This is why Vietnamese worshippers will visit different temples, addressing specific prayers to specific deities. A business request might be submitted to a successful mandarin, a family problem may be submitted to the Mother, etc.

Beliefs and superstitions

DON'T underestimate the extent and power of popular beliefs in Vietnam. The 'respect' mentioned a few paragraphs above will be more difficult to bestow when it will adversely affect your plans, but that's when it will be most needed. Your Vietnamese friends might not want to start a journey on a particular date and may be too shy to tell you the real reason why... it's simply not a 'good day' to travel. They might be 'very busy' the night you decided you wanted to go and try dog meat... it's not the proper time of the month to eat dogs. They might delay the purchase of your motorcycle or the signing of a contract because it's a 'bad day' to do business...

Kitchen gods and village spirits

Vietnamese religious beliefs are rich and varied. The afterlife is also modelled along the same lines as the earthly one, with the family theme being all important.

In all Vietnamese homes and pagodas, you will find an altar dedicated to the ancestors. Filial piety and family cohesion do not end with the death of a parent. Anniversaries of death are much more celebrated than dates of birth and give rise to family reunions and elaborate dining. Occasionally, you will be invited to such ceremonies.

If you do not wish to attend, simply refuse politely; otherwise, enjoy the discovery. A small gift (flowers, fruits, wine) should be offered to the host family.

DO take advantage of these invitations to discover more about local customs.

DON'T be shy, simply be respectful.

The family altar, or simply the sidewalk in front of the house, will also be used to celebrate other deities' anniversaries or special days. The polytheist religious system is a complex mixture of gods and real-life ancestors. Foremost in the spiritual hierarchy is *Ông trời* (literally, Mr. Heaven). At the helm of the universe, he presides over human fate. Next to him are other deities such as the God of Earth, the God of Water, the God of Mountains, the Kitchen God, etc. Each will have his special day of worship where joss sticks and paper offerings will be burned in the family's homes or at the temple. Prayers specifically tailored to the celebrated deity will be recited and offerings of fruits and alcohol will be laid on the home altar or at the temple.

In practically every village, there will be a temple to worship the tutelary spirit who founded the place. His death anniversary will be celebrated with numerous offerings at his temple.

But not all spirits are good and benevolent. Ghosts and bad spirits also thrive in the land of the dead. Most Vietnamese are quite afraid of evil spirits and many will have 'true' stories of encounters with living dead creatures.

Occasions for religious ceremonies are nearly endless; a more exhaustive list can be found starting page 161, Holidays and Festivals.

GOVERNMENT
& POLITICS

Vietnam

Government structure

The National Assembly is the governing body of the Socialist Republic of Vietnam. The country's President is the Head of State. The executive branch (i.e. the Government) is composed of People's Committees at provincial, district and communal levels. The legislative branch, also represented at each administrative level, is composed of elected People's Council. The People's Court, present at provincial and district levels, form the judicial branch. Vietnam's system is rather unusual, as it comprises yet a fourth branch called the Supreme People's Procuracy. It is a one-party state with the Communist Party reigning supreme.

If public management and political science are your cup of tea:

DO ask all the questions you want but always show respect for the country's institutions.

DON'T expect all Vietnamese citizens to know or be able to explain all of their institutions. Just think how many people in your country would be able to describe the political system that governs them.

DON'T indulge in the 'good guys-bad guys' bipolar view of the world. Reality only comes in shades of grey. And when you catch yourself dividing the world into two categories, 'Communists' and 'non-Communists', ponder the following definition:

"Capitalism is the exploitation of man by man
Communism is the opposite"

(source unknown)

And all other political systems we could add, are a blend of these two.

Myths and misconceptions

Because of its tumultuous history and especially because of its 'communist' label, Vietnam reaches deep into the emotional and other subconscious levels of most Westerners. And although the country has changed tremendously since the end of the traumatic American War in 1975, myths have endured, fuelled by the lack of exchange and communication between Vietnam and the Western world.

However, most myths do have some past or present elements of truths, so in order to help you separate exaggeration from reality, here are a few pointers:

Vietnam is littered with mines and leftover war ordnance.

Tell Auntie not to be afraid. Chances that you would step on an unexploded mine are extremely slim. Yes, people do still die from UXO... but most are metal recyclers that dig deep to find the last scraps of metal left. They usually get blown to pieces while trying to saw open live bombs. Unfortunately, children playing with newly found 'toys' are also prime victims of UXO. See page 61, The Wars, for more details.

Vietnamese must still hold grudges against Americans and Westerners.

Vietnamese have a saying that roughly translates into "let bygones be bygones". Of course not all individuals think alike but you will find very few people, including those who have directly suffered from the American War or who have lost friends and family, who will hold grudges against individual travellers. Most Vietnamese also make a considerable difference between individual Western travellers and Western governments.

Vietnam is governed by a handful of old but omnipotent leaders.

Vietnam's leaders actually retire before dying on the job. Of course, you wouldn't find any forty-year old in the three most important positions (the current President, Secretary General of the Communist Party and Prime Minister are all in their sixties) but they become 'advisors' to the government and leave room for younger players well before they reach 80.

As for the actual distribution of power, the Communist Party's politburo holds the lion's share. But it's a complex system where business, army, national security, and politics intertwine. Not to forget the Vietnamese people... you'll be surprised at how much people 'vote with their feet', choosing to comply or not with the different decrees and directives coming down from their government.

The Vietnamese way is always to try and reach consensus. For any directive to be implemented, it needs the support of all implicated parties. Consensus is sometimes reached only after arduous if not bitter internal struggles, but only the accepted results are then presented publicly.

Vietnam is a very poor country.

Well, this one's true. Vietnam is still one of the world's poorest countries. In fact, in 2001 it ranked 120 amongst 190. However it is engaged in a race to climb the ladder. During the 1991-2000 decade, the country's GDP growth averaged 7.5 percent. Even more impressive is that it managed to channel a major portion of this new wealth to the poorest households. By 2000, the poverty rate had been reduced to two-thirds of the 1990 rate. The international community considers that Vietnam can boast one of the best performances in terms of poverty reduction.

At the same time, Vietnam's Human Development Index is higher than expected, ranking 101, a hefty 19 places above its economic index. That means that the country has done much better than other nations of the same wealth. In comparison, countries such as the USA, Kuwait, Switzerland all have HDI rankings lower than their wealth rankings.

Vietnam doesn't look like a poor country.

Remember that 80 percent of the population live in the countryside. Most visitors will only see the more developed urban and touristy areas. Furthermore, with the liberalisation of its economy, Vietnam is also experiencing a widening gap between the richest and the poorest sectors of its population.

Another element that contributes to hide the extreme poverty experienced by a large sector of the population is the overwhelming generosity of the people. If you are invited to a farmer's household, you will be served a meal that the family probably has not and cannot enjoy more than a few times a year.

In such circumstances, it is better to eat lightly - a refusal would be considered impolite - in order to prevent the family from suffering long term consequences of their hospitality.

Being a communist country, most people obviously live terrorised or brainwashed by their political leaders.

If that's your idea of Vietnam, do come and have a look. It's come a long way since 1975. You will find more (real, not faked) smiles per capita, more optimistic youth, more national pride than in most countries. If there was such a thing as an 'optimism index', Vietnam would certainly be at the top of the list.

Communist propaganda is everywhere... including in those loudspeakers that blast you out of bed at five in the morning.

Not knowing the language, most Westerners have been brainwashed to believe that every loudspeaker and every billboard spews out political propaganda. The fact of the matter is that, as annoying as these loudspeakers may be, especially at the crack of dawn, their content is that of most community radios and rural programming around the world. Items such as agricultural programmes, health and child care issues, and daily community news (announcing water cuts, pipe repairs, closed streets as well as local activities and a slew of 'social publicity' aimed at educating people on safety and traffic rules, parking regulations, use of sidewalks, etc.)

Respect, as anywhere else in the world

Everywhere you travel, politics and national issues can stir very emotional responses from citizens. Vietnamese are not particularly sensitive but certainly are proud of their achievements and highly nationalistic.

DO show respect for other's opinion, no matter what's your own stance on the matters.

DO understand that not all people share the same political views.

Uncle Ho

Above all, **DO** show respect for the country's most illustrious leader. No, you won't be militarily escorted out of Vietnam for stating your personal opinion on Ho Chi Minh, but you certainly won't make many friends by showing disrespect for this national hero. It's one thing to criticise your own leaders but quite a different one to have strangers come to your country and criticise its leaders, ideology and institutions. It invariably arouses mistrust and negative reactions.

DO take time to find out a bit about Ho Chi Minh's life. He is undoubtedly an important political figure and, above and beyond the portrait that was relayed to us by our own media (the evil eyed, long nailed, never-to-be-trusted enemy of the free world), lies an interesting flip-side story. Books and museums abound depicting the long struggle of the Vietnamese towards independence from colonial powers, starting with Hanoi's Ho Chi Minh Museum, entirely consecrated to the life of Uncle Ho.

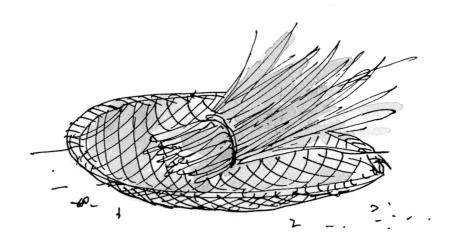

THE NORTH
& THE SOUTH

Vietnam

Differences in culture, language and mentality

Vietnam is a single country but regional variations in history, language, mentality, and culture are important. In a nutshell, most people will agree that the Northerners are more focussed on traditional values while the Southerners are generally more open to new ideas and are more business savvy, at least in a market oriented way. In accordance with this broad generalisation, Hanoi is the country's capital and political centre while Ho Chi Minh City (HCMC) and the southern provinces in general are the country's economic powerhouses.

Religion-wise, Northerners practice a more diluted form of Buddhism with stronger influence from Confucianism and traditional beliefs. The religious canvas in the South is more varied with a more traditional form of Buddhism coexisting alongside Catholicism, Caodaism and other faiths such as the Hoa Hao.

Hue in central Vietnam was once the country's capital. This area has kept very strong traditional ties with its glorious past. Nobility, sophistication and culture are the pride of its inhabitants.

Food: the good, the bland and the exotic

De gustibus et coloribus non disputandum (you can't argue about tastes and colours) said the ancients. Sure enough, each region, if not each city, in Vietnam will boast they have the best cuisine and will invariably compare all others to theirs.

Our own preference goes to the central cuisine, with

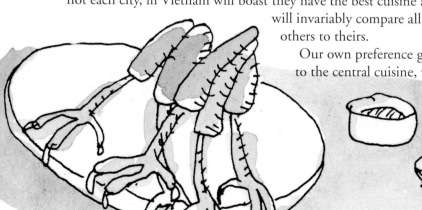

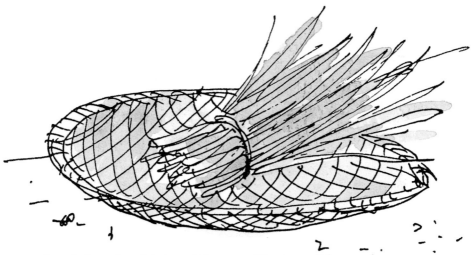

its subtle and sophisticated flavours. Northern dishes tend to err on the bland side, while the Southern recipes are a bit heavy on sugary tastes. But don't take our word for it...

DO make your own culinary discoveries, see page 95, Sleeping and Eating, for a list of exotic dishes you shouldn't miss.

Civil war aftermath

Beyond mentality, culture and food, political opinions and war history still distinguish the North from the South. Experience shows that civil wars leave scars that take up to a hundred years, or at least one whole post-war generation, to heal.

The Vietnamese may be very good at letting bygones be bygones, but one can still feel the tremendous gap that separates North from South. Many people who supported the losing side still harbour mistrust, resentment and even hate towards the ruling party.

DO ask questions if the subject is of interest to you but respect people's silence if they would rather not relive painful events.

DO avoid taking sides in a battle that wounded all sides and left the country free from colonial powers, but devastated. The future of Vietnam lies ahead. Numerous talented leaders and managers from all areas of the country are trying to lift it out of poverty. More than half the population have never known war and in a few years they will hold power. The transition from a post-war era to an era of baby boom and economic boom will have been completed.

CITIES & PROVINCES

Vietnam

Administrative divisions

Vietnam is divided in 64 provinces, including 5 cities with 'provincial' status (Hanoi, Haiphong, Danang, Can Tho and Ho Chi Minh City). Provinces are further sub-divided in districts, then communes and villages.

The governmental structure (ministries and mass organisations alike) is replicated at each level down to the commune, the last official administrative level.

Each province is headed by a People's Committee (the executive body of the National Assembly) composed of representatives from ministries and mass organisations. The main mass organisations are the Communist Party itself, the Fatherland Front, the Women's Union, the Farmer's Union and the Youth Union.

The urbanites and the country folk

DON'T be misled by the apparent modernity and sometimes Western-imitating looks of some urban youths. Eighty percent of Vietnamese are still rural folk. If you travel outside Hanoi and Ho Chi Minh City, you will discover the still predominant importance of tradition.

DO adjust your lifestyle and appearance in accordance with the local situation. What is acceptable in the backpacker's enclave of Pham Ngu Lao Street in Ho Chi Minh City is not necessarily acceptable in more rural settings.

Climate zones

Stretching 1,650 km from North to South (7 degrees of latitude) and from sea level to mountain tops (the highest peak culminating at 3,143 m) on an east-west axis, Vietnam obviously has a wide range of climatic zones. If you're coming to Vietnam with only shorts and a swimsuit... think again: the country is not all tropical in the 30's with a refreshing sea breeze.

From North to South...

Sa Pa A cool retreat from Hanoi's torrid summer temperatures and the closest you can get to seeing a few fleeting flakes of snow in winter.

DON'T forget your sweater, even summer nights can get cool up there. January and February are the coldest months with a slight chance of seeing snow. The best time to visit is from March to May, or September to mid-December, although autumn is much rainier.

Hanoi Hanoi has 4 distinct seasons with a hot and humid summer where temperatures can reach 40°C and a surprisingly cold and humid winter that can chill the bones of even snow-loving Northerners. Granted, the temperature rarely drops below 8°C or 10°C (the minimum is 5°C) but with a constant drizzle, a sauna-high humidity index and grey skies, it turns unheated cement houses into freezer-like boxes and gets most resident expatriates writing home for their favourite long-johns, woolly hats and duffel coats. Mid-January to mid-March can be quite depressing with a near total absence of sunshine (sometimes only two or three short appearances in a whole month) and a fine drizzle called rain dust by Vietnamese. The average of sunshine during the Hanoi winter is 1.2 hours per day... you get the picture?

The most pleasant seasons are spring (March-April) and autumn (October-December). July and August boast about 340 mm of rain per month compared to a low of 22-35 mm for December to February.

SAPA

HN.

HL.

H.

NT.

HCMC.

Halong Bay No doubt you'll want to go and discover this extraordinary UNESCO World Heritage site. The best times to visit the bay are spring and autumn. During the summer months, occasional devastating typhoons sweep across the northern coastline.

Vinh Granted, this city is not a favourite of most travel guide writers, but weather-wise, it does have one

important asset: its beaches boast the best wind conditions of the country. Who knows, in a few years it might become a windsurfer's and kite-surfer's paradise.

Hue Hue must have meant rain in some ancient dialect... your memories of the Imperial City will probably include a few heavy showers or never-ending drizzle. At the first signs of rainfall, an umbrella is probably a wise investment.

DON'T wait for the rains to stop before you go out and explore the city's beauties unless you plan to settle there permanently. More scientifically, annual rainfall averages 2,890 mm, compared to about 2,000 mm for most of the country.

Danang Even if only a short distance from Hue, Danang seems to be spared some of the heavy rainfall of its sister city. An umbrella is nevertheless a most useful article... for rain or sunshine.

Dalat Developed by the French as an escape from Ho Chi Minh City's heat, Dalat is always surprisingly and pleasantly cool in summer, especially after

sunset. Temperatures never exceed 20^0C, hence its other name: the city of eternal spring.

DON'T forget a sweater, even in summer. Nights can be quite cool, especially on a motorbike. As for winter, temperatures can drop to 10^0C.

Nha Trang This is beach-bum country where parasols and deckchairs sprout from the white sand under feathery coconut trees nodding in a fresh ocean breeze. If you can't handle this weather, you're a member of a rare breed.

HCMC The biggest city in Vietnam is under a typical dry/monsoon temperature regime, with a rainy season from May to November and a dry season from December to April. Temperatures barely fluctuate between an average of 32^0C during summer and 28^0C during the winter months. Don't be misled by the term dry season. The average humidity is 80 percent. As for the rainy season, it is characterised by daily short but heavy downpours. Monthly averages are above 300 mm of rain from June to September with January to March being the driest months with about 3 to 15 mm.

Can Tho The sun shines all year round in the Mekong River Delta and there are no winters. However, the region is flood-prone, especially between August and October when the mighty Mekong bursts its banks to inundate the fertile delta.

THE WARS

Vietnam

The long struggle to end colonialism

The first words that spring to the minds of many first-time travellers to Vietnam are *Vietnam War*. As obvious as the appellation might seem to Westerners, for the Vietnamese, *Vietnam War* could mean the one against the French, the Japanese, the Americans, the Cambodians or the Chinese.

For most Vietnamese, the American War (as it is more appropriately called here) was only one struggle in the 128 years of fighting to free their country from colonial rule or protect its borders. In fact, since the first military incursion of the French Navy at Danang in 1847, the country has not really known peace until a few conflicts after the fall of Saigon to the communist troops in April 1975. After the reunification of the country in 1975, Vietnam fought 2 more battles, first in Cambodia and then with the Chinese along its northern border. Peace really only started in 1979.

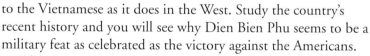

DON'T be surprised if the American War doesn't seem to be as important to the Vietnamese as it does in the West. Study the country's recent history and you will see why Dien Bien Phu seems to be a military feat as celebrated as the victory against the Americans.

The Vietnamese very often say: "Let bygones be bygones". Most people see no point in dwelling on the past or in nursing resentment. And with the newfound prosperity, all eyes are turned towards the present and the future.

DO understand however that they remember the suffering, the losses of dear ones and the deaths in their families. Most Vietnamese will also remember the nationalistic fervour, the ideals they fought for and the family values. Many who lived through the wars are nostalgic and sad that selfishness seems to be replacing traditional values.

The war legacy

Namstalgia, as wartime photographer Tim Page calls it, is the more visible lingering effect of the Vietnam Syndrome. Travellers, mostly American, still flock to Vietnam expecting to see the remnants of war at every street corner. The fact is, quite fortunately, most of the visible effects of war have disappeared from the daily scene. What is left, and there is enough to satisfy the *namstalgics,* will be found in museums, in preserved sites, in airports or military compounds and in geographically limited areas where unexploded ordnance is still being removed or where Agent Orange is still present.

What's left to see

Museums

The War Museum (Hanoi)
The Women's Museum (Hanoi)
The B52 Museum (Hanoi)
The Ho Chi Minh Museums (Hanoi & Ho Chi Minh City)
War Crime's Exhibition (Ho Chi Minh City)

Revolutionary Museum (Ho Chi Minh City)
Reunification Hall (Ho Chi Minh City)

Interesting sites

Dien Bien Phu
The Demilitarised Zone or DMZ
Duong Truong Son or Ho Chi Minh Trail along with the
Truong Son National Cemetery
The Cu Chi tunnels

At airports

As you taxi down the runway at Tan Son Nhat airport
(Ho Chi Minh City), you can still see the concrete half-tunnel-
shaped aircraft shelters along with a few antiquated aircrafts and
helicopters.

In Nha Trang, the military airport is adjacent to the
commercial one and Mig fighters can be seen taking off, circling
the area and landing regularly.

In the countryside

Large US
army trucks
are still used
in the South.

Anti
aircraft guns
and missile
sites along the
coast of North
Vietnam
(although
most are still
off limits).

A few
concrete bunkers
dating mostly from the French period.

Other

Souvenir shops. In Hanoi & HCMC shops offer an incredible collection of genuine imitations of Zippo lighters with war logos, dog tags and other military paraphernalia. What would be even more interesting would be a visit to the shops making these 'antics'.

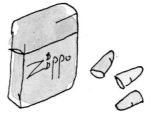

War toys. The fascination for war toys transcends cultural barriers. At the Hanoi airport, parents can buy their kids model replicas of American fighter planes, complete with US flags and other decals. In Ho Chi Minh City, recycled pop cans are used to create rather striking works of art ranging from metal baseball caps to helicopters.

What's more difficult to see

Reconstructed cities. Vinh, for instance, was so heavily bombed during the war that it really is a 'reconstructed city', albeit Eastern Europe concrete box style.

Agent Orange devastation. It is difficult to actually see the effects of dioxin on nature unless you have a trained eye for it. But a visit to any of the Peace Villages in Vietnam will expose you to one of the worst horrors of the war... the lingering and still devastating effect of dioxin on newborn babies.

Bomb craters are everywhere, but as most have been converted to fishponds, they cannot be easily recognised.

DO bring along any guidebooks you may have while visiting sites and museum. On-site explanations are scarce and mostly in Vietnamese.

DMZ Blues

After the defeat of the French at Dien Bien Phu in 1954, the Geneva Accords provided for the temporary separation of Vietnam into two parts at the Ben Hai River, near the 17th parallel. This separation was to last only 300 days until national elections would be called. As it happened, the elections were never held and with US military involvement, the temporary division soon became a no man's land, 5 km from either side of the demarcation line, known as the Demilitarised Zone or DMZ.

Along this stretch of land, running from the South China Sea (or Yellow Sea) to the Laos border, you will find some of the most widely publicised battle sites of the war: Khe Sanh, the Rockpile, Hamburger Hill, Camp Carrol…

DO take the organised tours from Hue to visit this area. They give good value and, because most of the sites have actually almost disappeared, you would have a hard time finding any of the locations for yourself. Most army bases are now tranquil rolling hills where, only after careful scrutiny, you will begin to discover the remaining bomb craters and scraps of leftover war paraphernalia. Agent orange's effect is quite visible, but again, one must be alerted to the fact that the bushy vegetation we see is actually a stunted vegetation growth where lush tropical forests once thrived.

DON'T expect to see much physical evidence of the American War. The campsites have practically disappeared with only a few trenches left or a barren plateau surrounded by bush-covered hills. However, not all UXOs have been picked up yet, so…

DON'T ever pick up unexploded ordnance, mines, detonators or other war leftovers unless they have previously been disarmed by professionals.

DON'T stray away from the beaten tracks to where guides indicate that the area is off-limits because of leftover unexploded ordnance.

Tunnel vision

The two most famous tunnel systems built by the North Vietnamese are Vinh Moc and Cu Chi.

The villagers of Vinh Moc were only a few kilometres north of the DMZ in what the US military called a 'free-fire zone'. Under the constant attacks of bombardiers and artillery, they switched from small family shelters to deeper dugouts. The red clay terrain provided excellent conditions and soon the entire 1,200 inhabitants permanently migrated from the surface to the 2.8 km tunnel system complete with kitchens, clinics, school, wells, ventilation shafts...

DON'T miss this site. The tunnels have been left in their original condition and size (unlike the tunnels at Cu Chi) and the local guides (essential if not to get lost in this underground maze) are knowledgeable and informative.

A visit to the Vinh Moc tunnel system might prove daunting for people with claustrophobic tendencies. And if you're not sure, it certainly will be a good way to evaluate your ranking on the fear-of-enclosed-spaces scale. A milder, but still fascinating experience is a visit to the Cu Chi tunnel system.

The site has been specially restored for tourists with a small cinema room, guides that will accompany you along the prepared circuit, displays of all types of traps used by the North Vietnamese

fighters, enlarged sections of tunnel to accommodate foreign tourists, examples of tanks and other military equipment and even a shooting range where you can try antiquated US, Russian and Chinese rifles.

The Cu Chi Tunnels

Construction of the first tunnels actually started under the French rule and spanned 25 years. The network is extensive, over 200 km of galleries in Cu Chi district alone. Other branches reach as far away as the Cambodian border. The network, built several stories deep, included living quarters, specially designed 'Dien Bien Phu kitchens' which diffused the smoke so as to be invisible from the skies, a weapons factory, command centres and even field hospitals.

Ironically, ignorant of the existence of the tunnels, US military installed a large base camp right on top of the network. It took them months to figure out why, at night, soldiers were being shot right in their tents.

The Americans and Australian tried a variety of methods to pacify the area around Cu Chi, at that time known as the Iron Triangle. But neither bombs, napalm, defoliant, hunting dogs, nor tunnel rats were successful in driving Viet Cong guerrillas away.

In 1969 the Americans decided to carpet bomb the whole area with B-52s, turning the area into what has been described as 'the most bombed, shelled, gassed, defoliated and devastated area in the history of warfare'. Although they managed this time to destroy most of the tunnel network, along with everything else around, it was too late: the war was ending and the tunnel had been an important component of the Viet Cong victory.

The Vinh Moc tunnels

The passages average 1.2 m wide and 1.7 m high. They were built on 3 levels ranging from 15 to 26 m underground. The deepest level was used by the Viet Cong fighters.

Each family occupied a small alcove-like chamber, excavated on either side of the passages. The complex included a central meeting hall capable of seating 150 people used, after the electrification of the tunnels in 1972, as a cinema.

It is said that 17 children were born in the underground medical clinic.

The Ho Chi Minh Trail

What was called *Duong Truonh Son* or the Ho Chi Minh Trail was actually a vast network of roads, trails and footpaths, changing course with seasons, bombing and the progress of hostilities. It was used by the revolutionary forces as a supply route for their troops and arms to reach the South. It ran parallel to Vietnam's coastline, high up in the Truong Son Mountains and also detoured widely through Laos and Cambodia.

Tens of thousands of Vietnamese soldiers lost their lives building, defending or using this vital supply route.

Currently, a new highway is under construction. It will link the entire country roughly along the same route as the historic war trail. Sections of the original trail can still be travelled mostly from the DMZ or from the Central Highlands.

Where have all the remnants gone...?

A decade ago, Vietnam's countryside was still littered with rusting war artefacts. Now, they are confined to a few isolated sites and museum displays.

The bulk of them were sent to the steel-rolling mills of Long Binh in the South and Hoa Binh in the North.

Many are now part of the newly rebuilt Vietnam as metal plates, girders and reinforcing rods.

Others have travelled abroad as metal ingots to be bought by former enemies Korea, Taiwan and Japan, only to come back to their homeland as Toyotas, pop cans and electronic equipment.

After having dug deeper and deeper to find the last remaining scraps, most serious metal hunters have now moved to Laos and Cambodia.

ENTERING
THE COUNTRY

Vietnam

Visa issues

Visas are still an expensive and rather tiresome aspect of travelling to Vietnam.

DO ensure that you apply for a visa well in advance. And if you do so from outside Asia, it may take even longer. Ask for a multiple entry visa (same price, but not always granted) or at least a double entry visa.

DON'T forget to arm yourself with a sheaf of passport photos: vital for visa applications and useful for other official dealings within Vietnam, where the photo booth is still a convenience of the future.

DO check for up-to-date information: regulations change frequently, as do visa lengths and prices. For example, there is talk of tourist visas being issued on arrival in Vietnam, falling in line with Cambodia and Laos, but at the time of writing, there is only an emergency possibility of having a visa delivered to the airport in Vietnam where you arrive. If avoidable, this is not recommended, as it is expensive and risky: many airlines refuse to fly passengers without valid papers, because they will be held responsible for flying you out again if there is a hitch and you don't get your visa.

Once you're on your way to Vietnam, usually on the flight or when you arrive at the airport, you will be asked to fill in an entry/exit form and to keep a (yellow) copy.

DON'T lose this form, you may need it to open a bank account or show an officious hotel receptionist and if you do mislay it, you may have to fill out another one before you can leave the country.

DO beware of the double dating system. Your visa will contain

WELCOME TO VIETNAM (BE PREPARED!)

a termination date and your passport will most likely be stamped with a permitted to stay until...date. These two dates are rarely identical! And, of course, the earliest of the two is the one that counts.

Working in Vietnam

More and more foreigners are working in Vietnam now. If you fall into this category or at least have paperwork to indicate that you do, it is possible to get one-year visas (though the first one may be a 'probationary' six-month visa). Your employing agency or Vietnamese counterpart will help you with the visa deliverance or renewal. A copy of your employment contract or an official letter from the company or agency is required for issuance and extensions.

Extending your stay

It is possible to extend tourist visas from within Vietnam. Contact the Immigration Police in Hanoi or Ho Chi Minh City. A long-term visa must be renewed, although, in special circumstances, it can sometimes be extended for a few days.

However, if you need to change visa category (for instance, from a tourist visa to a business visa or vice versa) you will have to leave the country in order to get the new visa issued.

Re-entering

If you plan to leave Vietnam during your visit, for example to visit a neighbouring country and then to return to Vietnam, **DO** make sure that it says multiple entry or double entry on your visa, or you will not get back into Vietnam without a fresh visa!

Land crossings

There are now quite a few Vietnamese land borders open to foreigners travelling to and from Laos, Cambodia and China, no doubt with more to follow. If you know where you wish to enter or exit Vietnam (other than at the three international airports in Hanoi, Danang and Ho Chi Minh City), BEFORE you apply for your visa, **DON'T** forget to specify these border crossings so that they can be added to your visa. Otherwise, you can have them added from within Vietnam, but with a little more hassle - and money, of course.

ON THE ROAD

Vietnam

Planes, trains and buses

Vietnam Airlines, the state carrier, provides a wide array of safe and fairly comfortable flights, both international and domestic. Things have not always been thus, but there is now a very trim fleet of modern, well maintained planes (mostly French and American: not a Russian Tupolev in sight), flown by well trained pilots. It's the safest driving you're likely to experience in Vietnam!

DO consider flying if you're going a long way within Vietnam, because any other means of transport is always much slower and sometimes only slightly cheaper.

DON'T get stuck in the mud: in the rainy season, road and rail are frequently flooded or even washed away in the regions that are hardest hit.

DO reconfirm any flight, as this is not a superfluous precaution in Vietnam.

DON'T arrive at the airport just in time for a domestic flight: your seat may well have been resold to someone else by then. Conversely, you might get lucky this way if all seats are previously declared as taken on a flight you want to take.

Until recently, it was actually more expensive for foreigners to travel from Hanoi to Ho Chi Minh City by train than by air. And this for a journey that still takes a couple of days as opposed to a flight lasting a mere couple of hours!

However, a dual pricing system is still in operation for air tickets. You get the same service, but it costs more because you're a wealthy foreigner. If you're not a Viet Kieu (see What's a Viet Kieu? page 6) and don't have papers to prove it, **DON'T** imagine that you'll find a way to get round this discriminatory practice:

you won't. The only loophole we have heard of concerns spouses of Vietnamese and Viet Kieu, who may be able to wangle a card somewhere entitling them to lower fares. But few things stay the same for long in modern Vietnam...

If what you're after is seeing plenty of scenery and having time

to meet people and chat to them, **DO** let the train take the strain. Trains are still very slow, despite reports almost weekly that they are picking up extra speed. Even the much touted 'Unification Express' crawls the 1,700-odd kilometres between Hanoi and Ho Chi Minh City. Trains are also surprisingly noisy and often rather Spartan, but they are still a very pleasant and civilised means of transport, with much more legroom than any kind of bus, and conserve some of the charm of a bygone era. On certain routes now, such as the trip from Hanoi up to Lao Cai (near Sa Pa) on the Chinese border, private companies are hitching refurbished carriages onto the regular trains. They offer - for a price - air conditioning, plush seats, comfy sleepers and gourmet food in a restaurant car.

Long haul buses are both the fastest and cheapest means of surface travel and are plentiful throughout Vietnam. If you board a bus full of locals (buses are usually full to bursting: they don't start their journey until they are), and manage to pay the local price, it should be dirt cheap. But foreigners often find themselves being squeezed gently into minibuses full of other foreigners. Unless you have the necessary language skills and tolerance for discomfort to track down and endure the local bus, these more expensive and more comfortable (and often air-conditioned) buses may be your best bet. The more reliable ones are operated by travellers' cafés such as Sinh Café and Kim Café and serve most of the bigger towns and sites deemed interesting to foreign tourists.

DON'T opt for the bus, however, if you're prone to claustrophobia, motion sickness, are pregnant, suffer from a weak heart or actually expect to have a good time. The Vietnamese are not renowned for the safety or courtesy of their driving, (see our Ten Tips to Surviving the Traffic in Vietnam at the end of this section) and road works, potholes, water buffalo and sleep-starved truck drivers abound.

Vietnamese people, especially young women, can be very prone to motion sickness. Unlike in Western countries, they have not been used since birth to travelling by car, train or boat.

DO use local city buses: once you've worked out where to catch the ones you want, these present an excellent (and stunningly cheap) way of getting around. Cities in Vietnam are investing in new buses and improving the service in an effort to combat traffic congestion.

Taxis, *xe ôm* and cyclos

Taxis are cheap and plentiful.

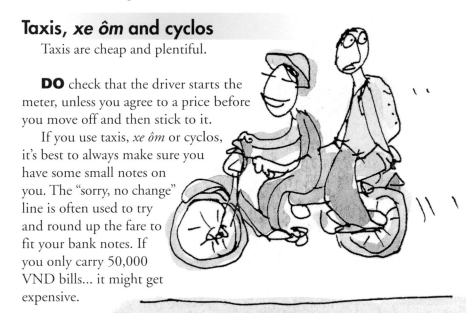

DO check that the driver starts the meter, unless you agree to a price before you move off and then stick to it.

If you use taxis, *xe ôm* or cyclos, it's best to always make sure you have some small notes on you. The "sorry, no change" line is often used to try and round up the fare to fit your bank notes. If you only carry 50,000 VND bills... it might get expensive.

DO make sure the driver has really understood where you want to go rather than just answering 'yes' to everything you say and then driving around aimlessly - with the meter running - in the hope that inspiration will strike from some unlikely quarter... If you can't make yourself understood, show your destination to him (or occasionally her) in writing. Nearly all taxi drivers can read, even if they can't drive.

A *xe ôm* is a motorbike taxi (*xe* is Vietnamese for 'vehicle' and *ôm* means 'cuddle' or 'hug'), a very popular and practical way of getting around. You'll find them on every street corner in the country - or rather they'll find you and eagerly offer their services. This is the fastest way to get across town without having your own bike and is often the best and cheapest way to get to a distant beach, village, site, airport, etc. Unless you're already an old hand at this game, **DO** fix a price before you hop on, politely ignore any attempts to renegotiate the amount along the way and check that you are indeed where you want to be before you pay off your *xe ôm*. No helmet of course, unless you're carrying one, but you do get to watch the world go by rather than threading through the traffic yourself.

Cyclos, or bicycle trishaws, offer a quiet, leisurely and eco-friendly way to cover short distances. A wonderful invention introduced by a Frenchman to alleviate the grind and degradation of rickshaw pullers, you will notice cyclo designs vary from one region to another. However, many city streets are now closed to cyclos, forcing them to make long detours. Unfortunately, they tend to lose much of their initial charm over time, because cyclo drivers tend to pester tourists and foreigners relentlessly and sometimes even aggressively.

DON'T take cyclos late at night, unless you know your way around. Numerous stories indicate that this is not a very safe option.

Car, motorbike and bicycle rental

It's great to be able to drive yourself in Vietnam and go where you want, when you want. For extra comfort but also for a price, cars, Japanese 4x4s and Russian jeeps can be rented for long journeys and to visit remote regions. But they usually come with a driver, and while he has the experience that you don't of the local stresses and dangers, he is not always very co-operative. Some diplomats and other expats have obtained Vietnamese driving licences and now drive their own cars, but cars, though fast on the increase, are really not the ideal form of transport for Vietnam's

narrow roads and saturated city streets. Renting bicycles and motorbikes is cheap and easy and this service is now offered almost everywhere in Vietnam. However, **DON'T** take the risks involved lightly: the number of foreigners implicated in traffic accidents - from minor spills to major, horrific trauma - is proportionately high, and this is a country with a soaring accident rate.

Why so? Because driving, roads, signs, lights and vehicle safety in general are a long way short of any kind of recognised standard.

DO check your travel or health insurance: while local medical care, particularly outside major centres, is rudimentary, foreign-run clinics in the cities are prohibitively expensive if you are forced to pay for them yourself.

DO take the time, if possible, to rent a bicycle for a few days before you rent a motorbike. This will allow you to familiarise yourself with local conditions without quite as much speed, risk and hot metal being involved.

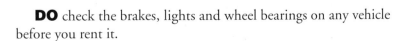

DO check the brakes, lights and wheel bearings on any vehicle before you rent it.

DO think carefully about the possible consequences of leaving your passport or credit card as a deposit for a motorbike. An imported Japanese machine is very expensive to replace if stolen or damaged beyond repair.

DO keep a sharp eye on your rented motorbike: a nice one is a very theftworthy item in Vietnam (rivalled only by mobile phones). And you wouldn't be the first sucker to have a motorbike stolen from you by the same person who rented it to you, who then debits your credit card for a fat sum or sells you back your passport for a tidy profit...

Although most travellers rank exotic infections as their number one fear, accidents are the single most important cause of death among travellers abroad, beating infection rate by 25 to 1.

Furthermore, if you worry about the dangers of non-sterile syringes or sub-standard medical facilities, accident prevention is still the most effective way to reduce these risks as well.

Minsking

The Minsk is a stylish, almost indestructible Belarusian two-stroke dirt bike with absolutely no frills attached, made in the town of the same name since the 1950s and the most popular of motorbikes imported into Vietnam from the former Soviet Bloc countries. There are a few 175cc versions about (like the ones still used in Cuba), but nearly all are now the 125cc model, which is ample for local road and trail conditions. Right up until 2002, Minsks were imported into Vietnam not as road vehicles but as farm machinery and are still widely used as such. Any Vietnamese city slicker would not be seen dead on a Minsk nowadays, so those that you see in town either belong to someone bringing a pig to market, or to a foreigner.

Out in the country, particularly in the mountainous north of Vietnam, is another story: there are Minsks everywhere, along with people who know how to fix them and a good supply of spare parts. Here, it is known affectionately as *the old buffalo* and carries impossible loads through some of the wildest of terrain imaginable.

Many expats and independent travellers find them the ideal multipurpose vehicle: cheap and easy to rent, buy, run and maintain, very stable if a touch heavy to manoeuvre in town, perfect for touring through the stunningly beautiful countryside. There's even a fairly comfortable seat with room for a passenger and luggage. And if you buy your own, they're very easy to sell when you leave Vietnam, probably for the same price you paid for it.

If you catch the Minsk bug, **DO** remember that the two-stroke engine will soon seize up and die without at least one part oil to 25 parts petrol (4 percent): you should always be able to see smoke coming out of the exhaust pipe (which explains why the Minsk doesn't feature in our section on eco-tourism...).

DO try kick-starting and stopping it several times over before you rent (or buy) a Minsk: once it's going, there's not much that will stop it, but you must be able to start it without too much hassle.

DON'T despair if it does die on you: if you still have petrol, it's probably only the sparkplug. Unscrew it with the special tool that came with the bike, clean it, check the gap with a penknife blade or similar (it should be around 7mm) and screw it back in. Still no luck? Put in a spare sparkplug. Nine times out of ten, this will get your Minsk going again.

DON'T buy any motorbike without some form of paperwork: it doesn't matter if it's not in your name, but without this you have no proof the bike is yours and you won't be able to sell it.

DO contact the Minsk Club, a loose union of (mostly expat) enthusiasts, based in Hanoi. They can help with finding decent maps, mechanics and up-to-date travel information. In Hanoi, they also occasionally organise Minsk repair workshops and some of the best parties in town. Minsk email: cuongminsk@yahoo.com or contact Highway 4 (84-4-926-0639), a bar and restaurant in Hanoi's Old Quarter with strong Minsk connections.

Walking

Nobody walks anywhere in Vietnam if they don't have to. Foreigners who actually profess a desire to stroll somewhere for fun are generally met with a mixture of incomprehension and disbelief from locals. This lack of local camouflage and obvious

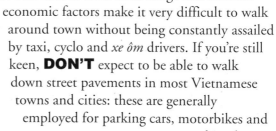

economic factors make it very difficult to walk around town without being constantly assailed by taxi, cyclo and *xe ôm* drivers. If you're still keen, **DON'T** expect to be able to walk down street pavements in most Vietnamese towns and cities: these are generally employed for parking cars, motorbikes and bicycles, displaying wares for sale, cutting hair, playing chess, hanging

out, etc. You will soon be forced to walk in the street and take your chances with the traffic.

Driving Licence

Technically, a foreigner needs a Vietnamese licence to drive anything above 50cc; while this is rarely if ever enforced, your papers won't be in order if you have an accident, whether it's your fault or not.

For short stays in Vietnam, your driving license from your own country should be sufficient, provided it applies to motorcycles. If possible, **DO** obtain an official Vietnamese translation of your license (unless it mentions that you are not entitled to drive motorbikes!). Official translations can be obtained at the public notary's offices in most large towns. It normally only takes a couple of days and a few dollars.

An international driving license is only a recognised translation of your own country's licence. However, if you look closely at the document, you will probably find that the Socialist Republic of Vietnam is still not part of the list of signatory countries. Nevertheless, any official-looking, photo-bearing document can be an asset when negotiating your way out of a delicate situation with local policemen or authorities.

If you intend to stay in the country for longer periods and wish to do more serious driving, then you might want to apply for a local driving license. You will need quite a bit of patience for this and a hefty pile of papers and letters that will include photocopies of passport, visa, driving license and originals of your driving license official translation as well as a letter from your sponsoring agency (not needed if you are on a tourist visa).

DO remember that this driving license will usually only be valid for the same period as your visa! After that, you start the process over again! But experience will make the process much quicker.

Horns and helmets

Horns are heavily used in Vietnam: a motorbike still runs with no lights or little brakes, but if the horn doesn't work, the bike needs fixing. Drivers constantly signal their position and intentions by tooting their horns, some even when they are alone on the road. A growing number of bright young sparks have had the amusing idea of fixing a powerful car horn to a scooter, and there's one right behind you...

DON'T let it get to you: it's just how things are here. If you start screaming at people for blowing their horns, they will - with reason - simply stare at you in amazement.

DON'T forget to use the horn yourself when you drive - otherwise, how will people know you're coming? Seriously, it can be dangerous not to signal your presence audibly, since everyone else does.

Helmets are spreading fast in Vietnam, and are now supposedly mandatory everywhere outside big towns. It's a difficult law to enforce, but

DON'T use that as an excuse not to wear one: hospitals in Vietnam are choked with people suffering from head injuries or in comas after motorbike accidents.

DON'T buy a Chinese helmet: it might look as good and be cheaper than other imported makes, but it won't resist a serious impact.

Ten Tips to Surviving the Traffic

DON'T spend hours waiting to cross the street on foot: that constant tide of traffic won't stop until late at night, so

DO as the Vietnamese do: take the plunge and inch slowly across. Observe the Miracle of the Red Sea, as the traffic parts like magic, flowing smoothly in front of you or behind, meeting up again on the other side.

DON'T make any sudden or unpredictable movements: freeze if you have to, but never lunge

forward or backward towards the safety of the sidewalk. In fact, you can do just about anything, but do it with conviction!

DON'T forget, if you're riding or driving, to look where you're going - all the time: if you hit anything in front of you, then it's your fault.

DO give way to any vehicle bigger and noisier than yours. Trucks and buses are particularly dangerous: often old, sometimes unsafe and usually all over the road.

DO watch out for unfamiliar obstacles: water buffaloes,

rocks of various sizes, broken-down trucks, deep holes, people sitting in the road, missing bridges, girls in *áo dài* cycling five abreast, slow-moving mountains of farm produce, dog fights, impromptu football matches, piles of building materials - and almost no lights on anything at night...

DON'T hesitate to take evasive action - even if this sometimes means leaving the tarmac or coming to a dead stop.

DO try to avoid getting involved in one of the all-too-frequent minor accidents that plague Vietnam's roads (and the major ones as well, of course), but if you are unlucky,

DON'T lose your cool, in spite of the interference of the large and vocal crowd that may gather: try to settle things amicably and swiftly. Sometimes, paying a reasonable amount of money will save you a lot of hassle.

DO remember that the only rule is: you're not allowed to bump into anybody... irrespective of what they did or should have done, or of what the road signs or traffic lights were telling them to do. Some people still seem to think that anything red means forward, comrade!

PRACTICALITIES

Banks

The first thing to know about money in Vietnam is that nothing beats a greenback: the US dollar, as in many developing countries, now reigns supreme. Such is the irony of history.

DON'T let anyone force you to pay in dollars, however: the law states that you always have the right to pay in dong (Vietnamese currency). You generally get a better deal if you don't pay in dollars, especially for smaller purchases.

The banking industry has been rapidly modernised and service is improving - slowly. Here are a few pointers to ease your path back to your own cash:

DO take your passport with you (or at least a good photocopy if you can't take the original)! This applies to all dealings with officialdom. You won't get very far without it.

DON'T count on cashing travellers' cheques anywhere outside the larger banks of Ho Chi Minh City and Hanoi.

THERE'S VIETNAM DONG AT ATMS.

DO avoid unnecessary hassle (and we mean hassle) by having the travellers' cheques made out in US dollars when you buy them.

The good news is that cash points (ATMs) dispensing Vietnamese dong, until recently a rare breed, can now be found in smaller towns. Credit cards are also taking off, with more and more businesses, hotels and restaurants accepting them. However, some will force you to pay the card surcharge yourself: an illegal practice, but there you go.

If you've brought US dollars with you (and we recommend that you should bring some), **DON'T** change them on the street: even if you know the local currency well and are on the alert for any scam (and there are many), you may still get conned and you won't get a good rate.

DO change them at a jeweller's (one that sells gold) shop around and you'll get a better rate than at the (state-controlled) bank.

DON'T travel to remoter regions without cash (plenty of dong, plus maybe some smaller dollar bills to ease the strain on your wallet). If you ignore this warning, you may find yourself walking back to the city.

Other offices

Vietnam enjoys the unique heritage of a most dubious procedural blend, namely Chinese mandarin, colonial French and Soviet-style communist bureaucracies. Kafka, eat your heart out. If you have dealings with other offices of officialdom,

DO keep calm: be assertive, but polite - and keep smiling. Things take time, offices close early and often and you will only be told something if you ask the right question, so ask lots of them, until (you think) you have understood which hoops you have to jump through.

DO photocopy every official paper that comes into your possession, and carry them at all times, along with plenty of passport photos.

DON'T despair, though: things are getting better. Not so long ago, it took about 100 (one hundred!) different visits to official offices to register a foreign business concern in Vietnam. A new policy dubbed one stop, one stamp has lowered this figure dramatically.

Most offices open at 08:00 in the morning, close officially or unofficially from 12:00 (sometimes 11:30) to 13:30 and stay open until 17:00. Countryside hours tend to be shorter. It's always advisable to do serious bureaucratic work in the morning.

Communications (telephone and post)

The landline telephone system is remarkably efficient: direct dialling, domestic and international, a same-day free repair service (lines are regularly cut by storms, heavy rains and hungry rats), card-operated pay phones in most towns. The catch is that it is not cheap: long distance calls within Vietnam are relatively expensive and rates for international calls are extremely high, although the introduction of new internet telephone services means they are no longer the world's most exorbitant.

Mobile phones are cheap and plentiful with two local systems providing good coverage. If you decide to buy one (or bring yours with you), **DON'T** leave it lying around: the market in stolen mobile phones is thriving. If you buy one, make sure it isn't 'hot', especially if you pay the price for a new one...

The postal system is also quite good in Vietnam. Here, too, links with the outside world are heavily taxed, making international postage charges disproportionately high. Within Vietnam, however, the post is not only fairly swift and reliable but also wonderfully cheap.

A few pointers:

DON'T seal a parcel before you take it to a post office. You will be required to show its contents before you can have it weighed and priced. You must also open any parcel you receive from abroad. This is to check whether what is written on the little green customs sticker corresponds to the contents. It is also to help post office officials determine how much import duty you should pay, but this is far from being an exact science, so **DO** tell people sending you stuff to Vietnam that they needn't be too exact for the box marked "declared value" when they fill out that little green customs sticker. Better still, they should add one or more of the following: no commercial value, for personal use, used items, etc. This should save you some money to start with, but **DON'T** just pay up if the fee seems unfair: there's room for negotiation here, particularly if you've got plenty of time. If the contents of your package are unlikely to be of interest to the post office workers, you can always threaten to leave it there...

DON'T post a letter or parcel with real postage stamps on it (as opposed to a mark from a franking machine) until you've had them cancelled ('stamped') at a post office. If they're steamed off and used again, your post won't get very far.

DON'T send big parcels abroad if you can avoid it. If you travel to Thailand or another nearby country and can carry the contents that far, it'll be cheaper to send it from there.

The Internet

Although only a tiny minority of Vietnamese uses the internet, the service is now efficient and widespread. It is still relatively expensive to have your own connection, but prices have been falling and speed and reliability rising. Internet cafés are also quite cheap and are almost everywhere (as widespread as most other Asian countries). In very rural areas, try the main post office.

In theory, the Vietnamese government retains control of virtual traffic across its territory, with a system of firewalls and surveillance of emails containing keywords, etc. In practice, if you know what you're doing, you can find anything.

DON'T be fooled, though: you could well be being watched (and read): people who post anti-government or anti-social material from within Vietnam have been arrested and imprisoned!

Some useful numbers
(Available throughout Vietnam)

International operator	110
Police	113
Fire	114
Ambulance	115
Phone directory	116
Time	117
Check your own phone (ring)	118
Phone repair	119

New Internet telephone services

International calls	171, 177, 178

The Information services

Information on telephone fees	142 & 143
Information on mobile phone fees	900 & 151
General information:	1080 (toll)
Consulting services	1088 (toll)

The 1080 number is the equivalent of an interactive yellow page service, particularly useful for information on telephone numbers, addresses, government offices, businesses, etc. As for the 1088 number, this is a rather unusual telephone service. An army of operators, some of whom speak English, are trained to answer just about any question from the public. From family planning questions to marital problems, meteorology to tourist information, historical or scientific queries, the 1088 crew are able to deal with all reasonable questions. During World Cup fever, they were specially prepared for the event, answering important or trivial questions from previous game scores to the underwear colour of the most famous players. The fee for this comprehensive service is a modest 250 dong (VND) per minute.

SLEEPING & EATING

Checking-in and Checking-out

Vietnam now has a wide range of hotels from the very basic to five-star luxury. A hotel with a permit to accommodate foreign visitors is called a *khách sạn*; a simpler (and cheaper) hotel aimed at local custom is called a *nhà nghỉ*. Foreigners can usually get a room in a *nhà nghỉ* now, but while some are fine, others are real flophouses. With all the ageing state hotels now competing with international chains and private 'mini-hotels' (often a good deal: look for tall, thin buildings like modern Vietnamese houses), there is no shortage of rooms, so **DO** shop around. Look at a room before agreeing to take it, check the air conditioning or fan, verify the level of noise from the street and from the karaoke bar in the next room. Ask to see a cheaper/nicer/quieter room with a softer mattress and a bath (almost all rooms have a shower and toilet en suite), suggest they throw in breakfast or give a reduction if you are staying several nights, etc. If no agreement can be reached, head for the next hotel down the street. Either you will be called back (a low paying customer is better than an empty room) or you can get the same deal or better next door.

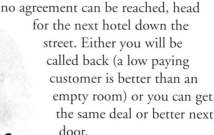

You will be asked (ordered, in fact) to hand over your passport at the hotel reception. Your identity will be carefully recorded, and, in some more far-flung or sensitive areas, your passport will even be taken on a visit to the local police station during the evening. Unfortunately, the same diligence is often sadly lacking the following morning, so **DON'T** forget to pick up your passport when

you check out! Many a traveller has had to waste a day's travelling or more in order to recover his papers. One way to avoid this infuriating situation is to carry photocopies of your passport. Some hotels profess not to accept them, so just say that you've left your passport behind to obtain a visa, to rent a motorbike, or similar: it might even be true.

It used to be almost impossible to stay at someone's house in Vietnam. This has been relaxed of late, but the owner should technically register your presence with the local police. Most of the time you will not even be aware of the paperwork (if any) involved. If you seek shelter in a remote or rural area, you will usually receive unhesitating and unstinting hospitality. In the morning, despite your hangover, **DO** give a little money or some food: it makes for a seemly token of gratitude, and you know that it's going to people who need and deserve it.

Dining out

Some behaviour in restaurants can be a little disconcerting. As soon as you sit down, you may be assailed by young ladies dressed in the livery of competing makes of beer. Their aim, surprisingly enough, is to get you to drink the beer they are promoting.

DON'T let yourself be pushed or rushed into anything: ask for the menu and take your time. After the menu arrives, the waiter who brought it will probably stand close by, expectantly awaiting your order or even reading out his recommendations over your shoulder.

DON'T be irritated by this, it is simply a manifestation of polite attentiveness.

DO notice that dishes are usually meant to be shared: everybody picks things up from the middle of the table and puts it into his own bowl.

DON'T protest if someone suddenly plops something down in your bowl: this isn't a mistake or a gag, it's a highly courteous gesture, offering you the most tender duck's foot or the crispiest pig's fallopian tube.

If you are eating out with Vietnamese friends or colleagues, especially if you are male, you will probably be expected to do a little drinking.

DO try to participate good naturedly, to the level of your abilities.

Although well aware that Vietnam is not a lingering culture, a local custom that both the authors of this book find particularly irritating is the snatching away of plates as, or even before, the last mouthful of food is removed from them. Again, this is probably only proof of service and efficiency, but if it is not firmly curbed from the start, your dining experience may not be quite as restful a one as you would hope.

Who picks up the bill?

If you are invited out to a restaurant, you are not expected to pay anything and may insult your host if you try and insist. Usually, one person pays for everyone.

DON'T forget, though, that if you suggest going to eat somewhere, you will be expected to pay for the whole group! Similarly, if it's your birthday, you've had a baby or moved into a new house, it's you who invites everyone else out for a meal.

DO check the bill before paying it. This is quite normal practice, even if you again have the waiter who brings it breathing down your neck. Extra dishes sometimes find their way onto the bill, or maybe something you ordered never actually arrived at the table.

DON'T leave a tip of 15 percent or even 10 percent: in theory, there is no tipping at all in Vietnam (after all, it is still a communist country), but in more upmarket restaurants, a small tip can be left in appreciation of good service.

For more adventurous stomachs

If it's unique culinary experiences you're looking for, **DON'T** hesitate to try some of these:

• Dog meat. Give it a go: it's not so bad, prepared in varied styles and washed down with a pleasant, sweet, milky coloured rice wine called *rượ chát*.

• Duck's blood soup. Served congealed with pepper, peanuts and herbs on top.

• Semi-incubated duck's eggs. They make an unusual but nutritious breakfast, served with slivers of ginger. Watch out for bits of beak or feather.

• Aromatic juice squeezed from cockroach-like insects called belostoma *(cà cuống)*, used to flavour some dishes such as rice pancakes stuffed with mushroom and meat.

• Beating snake's heart in rice wine. Not for lapsed vegetarians, this one.

• *Mắm tôm* the highly aromatic (or disgustingly smelly if you don't happen to like it) shrimp paste with pig uterus or other meats.

• Roasted chicken feet after a night out.

Endangered species

DON'T eat endangered species or their derivatives knowingly, if you can help it. In any case, most of them look much nicer than they taste. The usual justification for depleting biodiversity involves, rather paradoxically, improving virility and fertility. Things to avoid include:

• Bear meat and bear bile
• Sea horses
• Turtles
• Shark fins and shark fin soup
• Exotic meats such as tiger, pangolin (an armadillo-looking type of mammal also called the scaly anteater), etc.

• Wild snakes outside recognised (to the best of your abilities) snake breeding operations and also wild dogs...

Ten tips to eating on the street

DO sit down to eat at busy food stalls, not deserted ones: the food will probably be better there - and the atmosphere certainly will be!

DO go during local meal times (around 11h30 - 13h00 for lunch, no later than 20h00 for dinner): there aren't many refrigerators on the street and Vietnam is a tropical country, so if you prefer fresh food (and more choice), eat early.

DON'T wait to be served: look at what others are eating and point at something that looks tasty, or have a peek into the cooking pots and choose from there.

DO learn the Vietnamese words for *No monosodium glutamate!* (unless of course you happen to be an MSG junkie): just say *"Không my chính!"* with a smile when you order, and if it isn't already added, the chef may leave it out...

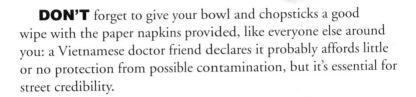

DON'T forget to give your bowl and chopsticks a good wipe with the paper napkins provided, like everyone else around you: a Vietnamese doctor friend declares it probably affords little or no protection from possible contamination, but it's essential for street credibility.

DON'T panic about hygiene - if you choose sensibly, your meal will not only be very cheap but also very delicious (as Vietnamese people often say). Safest of all are the vast array of filling soups and rice gruels. Deep-fried or boiled meat and vegetables are also a good bet.

DO use your judgement: for example, ice is usually made from purified water, but if you're outside the bigger towns or it's the rainy season, better not risk it. If you have a delicate stomach, avoid herbs and raw vegetables and only eat fruit that has been peeled. In fact, this last point applies anywhere if you're worried

about consuming pesticides, as they are showered over fruit in terrifying and uncontrolled quantities in Vietnam.

DO drink *bia hoi*: where available, this small beer (a weak, refreshing beverage, brewed daily and served chilled) is a safe, local choice and will help ease down almost anything!

DON'T stare at the pavement under your table (with a horrified expression on your face): it might spoil your appetite, as this is the natural repository for any garbage or inedible bits left by previous customers.

DO go back, if you like it: it can only get better, as the next time you'll be greeted with smiles, friendlier service and choicer morsels!

THE WELL-BEHAVED
TRAVELLER

Dealing with officials

Visa renewal, traffic accidents or simply getting stopped on the road by a policeman eager to get a closer look at a foreigner... sooner or later, you're bound to have to deal with Vietnamese bureaucracy and the administrative system.

Courtesy, patience and politeness are the keywords here. You can never radiate too much of these. Even when you reach the point where you're sure a good yell and a fist banged on the table will make things move... refrain. They may seem to make people move, they may relieve you from your frustrations, but they won't produce much positive result for you.

Remember, when things get rough, there are close to 80 million of them... how many are you? They have all the time in the world... how long will you be there for? They won just about all their wars, and they're awfully patient. You need them on your side if anything is going to happen.

Yes, it's true, sometimes a few small bills might help. Though this is usually when you have really done something wrong or when there is a fee for the service you are requesting. For instance: you run a red light with your rented motorbike. The policeman who stops you might not fit your profile of what a policeman should be or should do...

the above rules still apply. Be courteous, humorous if you can, but always respectful. You might be able to talk your way out of your mishap, but if you don't have the skills or talent, a small fine

will most likely get you out of trouble. Adjust the amount to the damage done. A simple red light wouldn't cost more than about US$ 2.00. It would be quite different if you had happened to knock down an old woman carrying a basketful of fruit.

DO be reasonable whenever you pay for anything... from a cyclo ride to a traffic fine. Other travellers will follow, they may not be as rich as you. Don't be a cause of inflation!

When dealing with officials, **DON'T** let them forget you. Be persistent. Many of them are simply nervous to deal with foreigners and would rather see you leave than deal with you. Turn that to your advantage. By always reminding them politely of your presence, they will eventually help you even if it's just to get rid of you.

DO go early for any administrative matters. Most things get done in the morning (ie before 11am) and afternoons are perfect timing for the "you come back tomorrow" line. Especially if the official thinks he won't be there tomorrow.

DO be prepared to come back a few times, however. Some transactions involve many different officials and the merry-go-round can take a few turns before it finally stops for you.

DO understand that the bureaucracy is not aimed at you specifically. All Vietnamese also have to go through these hoops.

DO consider yourself lucky... things have improved considerably over the last few years.

Environment

No matter what we like to be called, backpackers, visitors, travellers or tourists, all of us, individually and collectively, have a social, cultural, environmental and economic impact on the places we visit.

DO be aware of your impact on the environment and try to minimise it. Accept responsibility for the environment in which you travel.

Always leave all sites at least as nice and pristine as you found them.

There are ways to minimise the negative consequences of tourism while maintaining an enjoyable travelling experience with an abundance of happy memories to take home.

DO contribute, by your example, to a more sustainable tourism industry in Vietnam.

DON'T raise your expectations above reality. Electricity, plastic, television and modern clothing have the same appeal to all peoples. Accept the fact that cultures are not stagnant and people rarely think of themselves as being part of an open-air museum dedicated to the enjoyment of tourists. But cultures are more than costumes, dances and handicrafts. By looking beyond appearances, you will discover authenticity and tradition.

DO encourage eco-tourism, as it does provide a major economic driving force behind the conservation of natural resources.

DO help to conserve Vietnam's biodiversity.

Vietnam has a unique environment. It is home to one-tenth of the world's mammal, bird and fish species. Forty percent of Vietnam's flora grows nowhere else. Seven of the twelve large mammals to be discovered in the last century are from Vietnam.

DON'T consume wild meat or buy traditional medicinal products unless you are certain they are derived from sustainable management practices. As many of these products come from endangered or threatened species, in case of doubt, it is better to politely refuse. On the other hand, encouraging environment-friendly products does contribute to the conservation of wild animals.

DON'T buy souvenirs made from endangered plants and animals (ivory, tortoise shell, wild animal skins). Similarly, buying coral and ornamental fish helps maintain destructive harvesting practices.

You can make a difference!

You will no doubt realise that environmental awareness in Vietnam is quite low. By setting a quiet example and, even better, by explaining the reasons behind your actions, you can actually help change mentalities.

DON'T drop litter even if people tell you it's OK to do so. There are very few rubbish bins in the country, so this may mean you will have to carry it with you for a while.

If no toilet is available, be sure you bury your waste and all hygienic items far from waterways.

Never use soap or shampoo in rivers and lakes.

DO conserve energy whenever possible. Turn off air conditioners and fans when you leave your room.

DO remember that in Vietnam, national parks are not exactly what you would expect from ones you know back home. Most of them are really in the planning phase and exist only on paper. Some of them are actually poachers' paradises. None of them are equipped and organised for visitors like parks in Europe or America.

Culture

DON'T encourage the habit of paying local people to take photographs of them, as it encourages a begging mentality.

Never give money to begging children. It is far better to pay for shoeshines, postcards or books... even if you do pay a few dong more than the rock bottom price.

DON'T give sweets or chocolate. It will just make children's lives more miserable by adding dental problems to their already numerous health problems. When it is appropriate to give gifts, choose useful objects such as pencils, pens and notebooks, school bags or even clothing.

DO beware of anyone begging while carrying a sleeping child. More often than not, this is a scam. Children are rented and drugged to keep them quiet. Observe the locals. Who do they give money to? Most likely to the very old and to the handicapped. If you want to hand out cash, follow their example.

DO be aware that in some communities, it is still taboo to conduct an intimate relationship with a local. You will leave the country in a short time, but people left behind will bear the consequences for the rest of their lives.

Economics

DO encourage local products. Eat and drink local food, use local transport and local shops. Help turn tourism to the benefit of communities.

Some interesting addresses

Sustainable Tourism Resource Center
IUCN Vietnam
13A Tran Hung Dao, Hanoi
Tel: (84-4) 933-0012
Fax: (84-4) 825-8794
Email: tourism@iucn.org.vn

Tourism Concern
Stapelton House
227-281 Holloway Rd., London N7 8HN, UK
Tel: +44 020 7133 3330

Fax: +44 020 7133 3331
Email: info@tourismconcern.org.uk
Web page: www.tourismconcern.org.uk
The International Ecotourism Society
733, 15th St., NW, Suite 1000, Washington, DC 20005
Tel: +1 202 347-9203
Fax: +1 202 387-7915
Email: ecomail@ecotourism.org
Web page: www.ecotourism.org

Eco-tour suggestions

DON'T follow the crowd... get off the beaten track. Here are a few ideas:
• Visit Ba Be National Park, its lakes, waterfalls and rain forest (hntscbranch@hcm.vnn.vn).
• Go mountain biking in Dalat (langbian@hcm.vnn.vn).
• Sea kayak to uninhabited islands off Nha Trang, contact a local tour operator.
• Take an elephant trek in the Central Highlands (www.exotissimo.com or Dak Lak Tourist in Buon Me Thuot).

• 'Be a fisherman for a day' at Phan Thiet eco-tourist site.
• Discover the mangrove swamps of Vietnam's southernmost province: Ca Mau (Lam Vien and Vam Sat eco-tourist sites).

MAINLY FOR MEN

Sex, songs and massages

Sorry ladies, Vietnam is no doubt a man's paradise, even if only for the eyes. You are likely to see more charming smiles, graceful bodies and seducing eyes per square kilometre than in any other place on earth.

Although prostitution is rampant, in Vietnam even the dancing girls and the taxi girls (girls that you bring back to your hotel room) have retained an air of youthful naiveté and sincerity that adds to their already devastating charm.

But caution is always the best approach in uncharted territory. There is makeup and then there is life.

Karaoke and massage parlours are often the front door to more sleazy and personal services. But, under constant surveillance from the social evils police, many establishments are just what they advertise... places to sing and relax, albeit in the company of charming young and respectable ladies. The one thing to remember is that, except in the true-blue back alley clandestine bordellos, you can still go for a sing-along or a regular Vietnamese massage in any establishment that advertises these services. Extras are extras and never

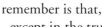

compulsory. *But they forced me into it...* is not such a good line for anyone who knows the scene here.

DO remember that prostitution is still regarded as a social evil, on top of being illegal. However, it is quite unlikely that you would get into any real trouble with the authorities, but you could be caught in an occasional police crackdown. Luckily, your foreigner (and guest) status will, more likely than not, save you from visiting the local judge. A small on-the-spot fee and disapproving stares and words are probably the worst you can expect.

DO be suspicious of anyone who says she loves you in the first ten minutes of conversation. Love has many meanings and always comes with responsibilities... in cash or in kind.

DON'T make serious promises you can't keep. Most Vietnamese ladies will be quite direct about their intentions, short term or long term, and in turn will try and hold you to your word.

DON'T carry too much cash when visiting bars and nightclubs. When overstuffed wallets are flashed in public, you never know who is watching. It could spell trouble a few hours down the road.

DON'T engage in unprotected sex. AIDS is spreading through Vietnam as fast as the country is opening up. And although AIDS is the number one word on everyone's lips when it comes to unprotected sex, there are also a number of other diseases that you might have to explain to a spouse or a partner when you get back home. Gonorrhoea, syphilis, trichomoniasis... if the disease doesn't kill you, someone else might.

DON'T get drunk alone in public places. Vietnam is a safe country, but do you really want to take the risk and become one of those rare crime victims?

DO report all crimes to the police. No, you won't find them particularly helpful or sympathetic, but in the long term, you will help improve the situation by not keeping silent.

DON'T ever abuse children. After Thailand and Cambodia, paedophilia is spreading to Vietnam. Be careful not to act in any way that could be seen as encouraging it.

Taxi girls and dancing girls

There are several ways to pick up sex as a gentleman, without bullying, deceiving or overly destroying the lives of your potential partners.

For someone in a hurry who does not know where to go, it is best to stick to the dancing bars, discos and other places where dancing girls, taxi girls and foreign-husband hunters mix with the normal crowd of fun seekers.

DON'T believe all what you are told... "It's my first time here", "I've just come to celebrate my birthday with a few female friends of mine", etc. Girls who hang out at discotheques are simply not your usual traditional family-oriented career-dreaming types.

DO negotiate the price first if you're going to pay for services. Beware of the "Oh, just anything you want to give me" price tag. It's bound to get more difficult than that when comes the time to hand out some cash.

DON'T be a transmission vector for the AIDS pandemic. It's bad enough as it is. It doesn't matter what the girl says, there's no such thing anymore as safe unprotected sex with a stranger.

DON'T have sex at all if you can manage it. Although prostitution can never be eliminated, it can be minimised. Young girls will not be dragged into the flesh business if demand is not there. Very few girls choose prostitution as a fulfilling career!

But what about true love?

Well it happens, sometimes. You wouldn't be the first foreigner to fall in love with a Vietnamese. If you are ready for the long-term commitment, it is fairly easy to get married locally, as long as you have a few weeks to spare and ways to retrieve all your important papers from your home country. The procedure will take a minimum of 5-6 weeks if both your paperwork and your future wife's are in order.

DO remember that Vietnam has laws and regulations about marriage and that no matter how much of a hurry you are in or how much you love each other, you will have to abide by these rules.

Family wedding and civil wedding

Remember the three pillars of Vietnamese society? When it comes to weddings, of course it's a family affair. The Vietnamese regard the civil marriage as an 'authorisation from the government to get married'. So strong is their belief in the 'family wedding' as opposed to the civil one that the government actually had to pass a decree forbidding the holding of the family wedding ceremony before getting 'the papers'. But be advised, those papers are the wedding. Once you've signed, you're as married as it gets.

But if your partner is Vietnamese, the fun has just begun. After the civil wedding will come the 'engagement' ceremony where elders of the groom's family will meet elders

from the bride's family in order to exchange gifts and secure the authorisation from both families to have their son/daughter married. - But they're married already! Maybe before the law, but not yet according to the traditions of a Confucian-based society. A 'good day' will then be chosen for the ceremony. It will be based on the lunar calendar and your respective astrological signs. It could be a few days after the engagement or up to a few months or even a year. Have we talked about patience yet?

The final ceremony will involve both families and a few hundred friends and colleagues. Once a banquet has been held for all these people then, yes, you are husband and wife. The engagement and wedding ceremonies are highly colourful and full of interesting rituals. It is not the purpose of this book to delve

into the
complexities
of these
Vietnamese customs.
Your future wife will guide you along this merry road.

However, here are a few basic survival tips... as if one would need more advice once one has chosen to get married!

DON'T think your foreigner status will exempt you from the government's regulations on marriage and family law. The Vietnamese are proud of their achievements in this sector and they will resent any condescending attitudes or remarks.

DON'T try to go faster than the civil servants handling your case... yes, it can sometimes be a bit tricky if you or your spouse don't have all the necessary papers. But do you really want someone to put the brakes on and give you a real taste of stalled bureaucracy? Most clerks will be polite and even helpful if you treat them with respect. A lifetime commitment is certainly worth a few weeks of patience.

DO remember that every culture has its customs which

most of the time can look quite bemusing to an outsider. This is not the time to look down on and ridicule your partner's beliefs and traditions. Just relax and enjoy the ride. You will find most people to be extremely helpful in guiding you through the rituals and explaining their meaning and importance.

DO believe your future wife when she presents you with delays or additional difficulties. Again, most people will really do their best to welcome you into their family, but problems do happen. Let the Vietnamese solve the Vietnamese problems.

DO be aware that Vietnamese women who go out with foreigners tend to be treated very badly by other Vietnamese. There is a natural tendency to believe that any - and especially any good-looking - Vietnamese girl who dates or marries a foreigner is a prostitute or bar girl. As sad as it may sometimes be, it is usually better to let the Vietnamese handle this between themselves. Intervening might make you feel better but it will quite surely make it worse for your partner.

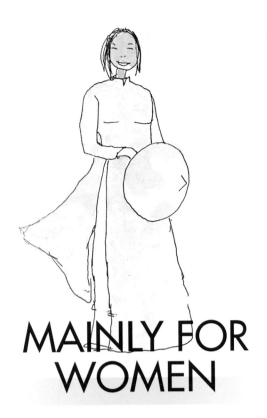

MAINLY FOR
WOMEN

Vietnam

Safety and curiosity

For foreign women, Vietnam is an easy country. You can walk around alone in complete safety at just about any time of day or night. Vietnamese men can be quite *macho* in the way they see the role of women, but they rarely apply this offensively to foreign women. You won't be whistled at, followed, chased after... except of course by the cyclos, postcard sellers and conical hat hawkers.

Even though Vietnam is probably one of the securest places on earth, don't tempt fate: as anywhere, a modicum of prudence and a splash of common sense are the order of the day.

DON'T wear your nicest gold jewellery at night;

DO keep your handbag tucked tightly under your arm, especially while riding in cyclos. There are a few grab-and-ride motorcyclists in the cities and they are fast.

For women travelling alone, the biggest problem will probably be curiosity (meaning downright nosiness sometimes), which comes with an avalanche of questions: "So where is your husband?", "Where are your children?" "But why aren't you married? How old are you, then?", etc.

The same applies to any single (or divorced)

woman over the age of twenty-three and a half. Living alone in this country is never understood as a matter of personal choice and will immediately foster bafflement and suspicion... and a barrage of questions!

Tight and see-through, but don't bare too much

With regards to what is considered the "appropriate" way of dressing in Vietnam, it is worth taking a closer look at the traditional costume, the *ao dai*. Although nowadays it's only worn by students at certain schools and during important occasions or at smarter evening parties, it gives a good indication of what is generally 'done' and 'not done' in terms of dress.

The first thing you'll notice is that the top is worn very tight and that it shows off the figure very well. Indeed, in contrast with many other countries where a woman's body must be hidden by reams of material or flowing garments that suggest nothing at all, close fitting clothes are not a problem here.

Moreover, especially when white, an *ao dai* gives a very good view of a young woman's underwear. It would seem that transparency does not necessarily go hand-in-hand with indecency!

However, with its long-sleeved top and trousers right down to the feet, this traditional costume covers a lot of traditionally shielded flesh.

In short, clothes can be as tight and diaphanous as they come... You can never wear too much, but don't bare too much! So, **DON'T** hesitate to wear body-hugging little tops, tight trousers or skirts... if you feel so inclined, of course!

DO risk a little lace and some see-through stuff sometimes: don't be straight-laced about it! The Vietnamese are not.

DO avoid plunging necklines, bare shoulders, short skirts, shorts... Very little naked flesh is shown in this country. Even though this practice is very rapidly becoming more flexible, especially in the larger towns where young Vietnamese women are adopting more and more international fashions, it is definitely advisable to conform to tradition if you travel in rural areas, visit pagodas and temples and if you are working in Vietnam.

DO show respect for local ways of thinking by adjusting the way you dress. Appearances are very important. Provocative attire and shabby, scruffy clothing are not recommended.

DO be advised that even though Vietnam is not a country where you risk being attacked for your immodesty, receiving reprimands or enduring direct comments, people will definitely look askance all the same, and there will be no shortage of remarks being made behind your (bare?) back... especially because people will often assume that you don't speak the language. And in fact you are often better off if you don't know what's being said!

Code of conduct

DON'T touch Vietnamese men in public unless you are absolutely sure it will not embarrass them and their entourage.

Aside from some very rare exceptions, Vietnamese women don't drink and don't smoke. (They're such saints...) It looks bad! But, as a foreigner, smoking shouldn't damage your image too much. The same goes for alcohol. In fact, most Vietnamese (well,

Vietnamese men) will encourage you to drink as much as them. 'Down in one' *(trăm phần trăm)* is a well entrenched custom.

Falling in love

Love can always strike on the path to the paddy fields, and there are numerous cases of happy endings sealed by marriage vows. (See our previous section for notes on Family wedding and civil weddings).

Mixed marriages involving foreign rather than Vietnamese women usually provoke less disapproval and salacious comments from other Vietnamese. But, **DON'T** underestimate the consequences! Vietnam is a very traditional society with regards to the role of women. While living in Vietnam, a foreign woman - even one with capital assets - will not enjoy the liberties that generally come with the status of being head of a family. Oh, and **DON'T** forget: you're marrying your mother-in-law, too! You should be aware that, traditionally, young married couples go to live with the groom's parents, where the young bride becomes a sort of slave to her mother-in-law for a while. Not many Western women these days would be keen to take on the role of Cinderella (even opposite a really cute Handsome Prince). This explains, in part, the striking disproportion in the (smaller) number of mixed marriages in this direction. Even though your status as a foreign woman can cut you significantly more slack, you will almost certainly suffer strong pressure - and intrusions - from your family-in-law.

DO commit yourself knowingly: your life will not be so simple if you don't want to have children, or if you don't become pregnant within the first three weeks after your honeymoon.

DO be prepared to receive many, many, many pieces of advice on how to bring up the children you will have had... Stay at home without setting foot outdoors for the first month after giving birth, swaddle the baby in piles of clothes (even if it's 45°C in the shade), sleep with the baby and the mother-in-law (your husband can sleep on the couch), etc., etc.

DON'T ever forget this, though: love may conquer all!

SHOPPING

Vietnam

Markets and minimarts

Shopping can be an interesting - but also a very exasperating - experience. So arm yourself with plenty of time and patience and get out there to find the amazing variety of great deals Vietnam has to offer.

DON'T miss the markets: among the most atmospheric in Southeast Asia and still the hub of commercial activity everywhere in Vietnam. Notable markets include floating ones in the Mekong Delta, Cho Lon market in the district of Ho Chi Minh City that bears the same name (it actually means big market), the large fruit and flower market in Dalat, any of the major markets in Hanoi, the colourful Sa Pa market and other ethnic minority markets in the mountainous north of the country.

DO go early when shopping at local markets. Goods are brought fresh every day from the countryside and without refrigeration they will suffer from the heat as the day drags on.

Shopping in many parts of Ho Chi Minh City is now little different from shopping in Bangkok or any other Asian metropolis. Commercial complexes and supermarkets are also sprouting up in Hanoi and other sizeable towns. Elsewhere things change more slowly.

Before full-blown supermarkets arrived in Vietnam, there were only minimarts: compact operations only present in the big cities, catering almost exclusively to a foreign clientele. Plenty of these little international stores still exist, stocking all kinds of surprising, exotic and expensive goods, catering to the hankerings of various expat groups. Over the years, caviar and Russian salmon have become scarcer, Fruit Loops and Californian Chardonnay more abundant. Still no real Marmite, though.

DO check the expiry dates carefully on any imported produce you buy: many of the more obscure items in these shops have been quietly gathering dust (not to say rotting away) for years.

In Hanoi, you may notice a baffling remnant of the city's old ways. Tradesmen as part of Chinese-style commercial guilds were traditionally grouped together geographically (as many have remained in the Old Quarter), but a more modern breed of shopkeepers, such as those selling televisions or making photocopies, often elect to bunch together in a similar way. The practical upshot of this is that you may spend several weeks in Hanoi, convinced that it is simply impossible for the moment to obtain, say, a tennis racquet. Then, one day, you will turn a corner into an unexplored street and be confronted by an entire row of shops selling nothing but tennis racquets.

Bargain, bargain, bargain

The idea of a fixed pricing system is still quite novel in most commercial contexts, which means that a little good natured haggling is an important habit to develop. Anywhere outside of supermarkets, restaurants and anything controlled by the state, bargaining is probably possible and usually essential.

The price of fresh goods can fluctuate quite a lot, depending on quality, season, availability, origin and type of goods. Mangoes for instance, come in many varieties from cheap and fibrous to expensive and juicy...Paying the lowest price might not always be the best bargain.

DO be warned that, as you are always easily spotted from a distance as a foreigner, you will be asked to pay more than locals. Sometimes just a little more, but often outrageously more, even if this is not always immediately obvious to you, especially when relatively small sums are involved. It might seem like a snip, but you may be paying ten times the going rate.

If you feel mean haggling over such small sums or are tempted just to pay up for a quiet life, **DON'T** forget to think of other people who will pass this way after you. You shouldn't be too afraid of offending local sensibilities: if you pay vastly over-inflated prices without a murmur, you'll simply be seen as the sucker you're letting yourself be taken for!

In order to hone your purchasing skills to a fine art, see our Ten Tips to Savvy Shopping at the end of this section.

Fake goods

Much of Southeast Asia is notorious as an earthly paradise for counterfeiters and Vietnam is no exception. Everything has been faked and flogged in Vietnam - from orchids to orgasms, via the Mona Lisa, motorbikes and MSG. At the time of writing, it is almost impossible to buy original music CDs, while copies of them are on sale down every street in town. This also holds good for software, frequently available in pirated form before it has even reached the computer stores in Europe or North America.

DO consider your motives carefully if you purchase counterfeit goods: if you buy a Rolex wristwatch for $20, you know that there is no chance of it being anything like a real one, except for its superficial appearance. If this is all you want, that's fine, but **DON'T** complain if you get searched at customs on your return home, have

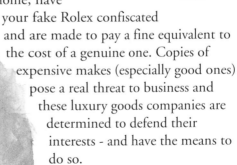

your fake Rolex confiscated and are made to pay a fine equivalent to the cost of a genuine one. Copies of expensive makes (especially good ones) pose a real threat to business and these luxury goods companies are determined to defend their interests - and have the means to do so.

Very good copies can be found in Vietnam, particularly items such as clothes, sports equipment and luggage. The Vietnamese are redoubtable and wily business operators, and both foreign and domestic companies often find it impossible to prevent know-how from leaking out. Even products made from materials imported exclusively find their way onto the local market at budget prices.

DO let the buyer beware however, it's possible to find excellent deals, but only if you really know what you are doing. You could end up with something that is a substandard fake - except for the label, which is entirely genuine - although that, too, was Made in Vietnam!

To some extent, you can argue that fake goods provide a measure of 'justice' for developing countries like Vietnam, where real luxury goods are produced with really cheap labour to be sold subsequently to affluent Western consumers. Most people in the countries where these products are made could never afford to buy them, but they can afford cheaper copies. When (or if) countries such as Vietnam become more affluent and develop closer trading ties with the richer, industrialised countries, pressure will be brought to bear (in fact, this has already begun) to ensure that such fakes disappear from the market.

What you pay for is what you get

As we have just pointed out, there're a lot of fakes in Vietnam, many of them good ones, so if you think you've found the bargain of the century, maybe, but maybe not!

DO be advised: for now, there is no trading standards authority in Vietnam, so check the quality of what you're buying very carefully, especially if there are safety concerns involved.

DON'T expect to get your money back if you change your mind after making a purchase, or even if you realise belatedly that the goods you have been sold are not as advertised... Check everything checkable yourself before you hand over your money. If it runs on electricity, get the assistant to plug it in and test it. Keep an eye on it while it's being packed or wrapped.

The dual pricing system

As in several other developing countries, particularly (ex-) communist ones, a dual pricing system has been in operation for some time. The good news is, this is changing.

Trains, which only a few years ago were as expensive for foreigners as flying, should now be the same price for all passengers. Inevitably, to meet the ensuing shortfall in revenue, the very modest prices charged previously to Vietnamese have risen steeply since everybody else began paying them, too. Air travel still costs more for foreigners, but the gap between foreigner and Vietnamese prices is narrowing.

The government has given all private and state-owned enterprises a few years to eventually wipe out the dual pricing system, including entrance fees to all heritage sites and other places of interest. This new regulation is gradually being introduced throughout Vietnam and should be universally observed within a couple of years.

A thornier problem for foreigners who elect to settle down and rent somewhere to live in Vietnam is that of utilities, namely electricity and water. Here, too, a dual pricing system has long been in operation, with hefty charges and inflated estimates of foreigners' rates of consumption. There is no longer any need to pay these extortionate prices; landlords no longer have to obtain an expensive permit previously necessary to have foreigners inhabit their property (they only have to register your presence at the local police station, equipped with copies of your passport and visa). You can always pay the local price for electricity and water, as long as the bills are in the Vietnamese house owner's name. However, many landlords see no reason why they should cease to profit from these lucrative extras (which of course have consequently become even more lucrative).

DO negotiate firmly if you want to rent a place: as a foreigner, you are a good prospect, since you will almost certainly pay more than a local, you won't start worshipping your ancestors in the house and refuse to ever move out - and you may even attract other monied foreigners to the neighbourhood. However, you should also be aware that there is no legal protection for people renting accommodation: if you have a problem, you must solve it with your landlord - again, through negotiation.

The pleasant - and unusual - result of all this is that, in many respects, Vietnam has actually been getting cheaper (only for foreigners, though) over the last few years: not many other countries in the world could say the same!

Ten tips to savvy shopping

DO always ask around to get an idea of basic prices: a ride on a motorbike, a plate of fried noodles, a packet of cigarettes, a kilo of mangoes, etc. For more important purchases, try and get a local friend to go along with you, or better still, let him do the buying without you: prices are often lower when foreigners aren't around.

DON'T feel awkward or rude about bargaining: everyone bargains in Vietnam and you'll look like a green tourist if you don't.

DO insist on being quoted a price as soon as you start showing interest in a commodity or requesting a service. It's too late to ask once the silk shirt has been wrapped or after your bike has been fixed. This first price is your starting point and it's quite probably too expensive, so

DON'T look happy or resigned to paying what you're asked: always begin by showing your gentle disapproval, tut-tutting or saying something like: *Đắt quá!* (Too expensive).

DO consider various bargaining options, not just a straight fight over figures. If you buy several, the price should come down. Ask them to throw in some small extra you would like, for the same price. If you are quoted a price in US dollars, ask how much that is in Vietnamese dong and try rounding it down. Be forewarned, though, that the concept of the special offer is still in its infancy here (like 1 percent off if you buy a truckload)...

DON'T hesitate to walk away if you cannot agree on a price: either they'll come after you or you'll find the same thing on sale somewhere else.

DO stay Zen... Shopping can be quite a rodeo when you're surrounded by eager stallholders all shouting, smiling, waving and pointing at their wares.

DON'T buy antiques to take home unless you're confident you can get them out of the country. The law prohibits their export, but remains vague as to what exactly constitutes an antique.

DO buy ethnic minority products directly from ethnic minority people, if at all possible, rather than from shops run by ethnic majority merchants, who often exploit their suppliers ruthlessly.

DON'T expect to get the better of any deal: Vietnamese have boundless reserves of experience and patience in doing business. You stand little chance of matching them!

Good buys in Vietnam

Lacquer ware
Ceramics Painting
Woodblock prints
Silk
Clothes in general
Embroidery
Carvings (stone and wood)
Precious or semi-precious stones (such as jade)
Jewellery
Rugs

TREKKING

Vietnam

Off the beaten track

If you want to visit rural villages and ethnic minority areas, trekking is one of the best ways of getting there - sometimes the only way. Most of the best places to go hiking are in the mountainous north of the country, but there are also interesting places to trek in the Central Highlands and it's even possible down in the Mekong Delta. Trekking is also possible in some national parks, such as Cuc Phuong (a few hours' drive south of Hanoi) and Cat Ba (on the island of the same name in Ha Long Bay).

Many visitors to Vietnam wishing to stretch their legs flock to Sa Pa, a charming little town in the far north, perched in the mountains near the Chinese border (called the Tonkinese Alps by the French, who built Sa Pa to escape the summer heat in Hanoi). Sa Pa is still a good base for trekking in the region, which is home to a rich array of ethnic minorities.

Above Sa Pa, often shrouded in cloud, towers the Phan Xi Pang (or Fansipan), almost 3,200 metres above sea level and the highest point in all of what was once called Indochina. Climbing this is probably the ultimate sporty trekking option in Vietnam, but not necessarily the most interesting, because above the foothills it is just rather bleak jungle. A strenuous climb, it will take you

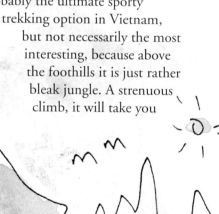

from two to four days, depending on weather conditions and on your physical condition. If you make it to the summit and are lucky that the cloud cover lifts for long enough, you may get a stunning view, allegedly stretching right down to the South China Sea.

DON'T plan to climb the Fansipan from May to August inclusive, unless you like leeches and landslides.

DO take warm, light clothing with you: this is the only place in Vietnam where it very occasionally snows.

DON'T go it alone: this is rough and wild terrain, with no inhabitants (apart from the odd wild animal that hasn't been hunted yet) and no back-up. A British teenager died from a fall on the mountain not long ago.

DO take a guide with you, preferably from the Black Hmong ethnic minority. They are one of the local indigenous peoples here who know this terrain better than anybody and need your money more than the ethnic majority Viets (or Kinh). A guide is essential, because there are barely more than hunters' tracks on the mountain and everything (tents, food, clothing) must be carried up with you.

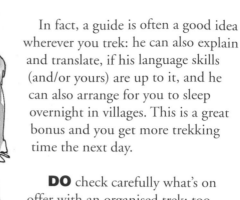

In fact, a guide is often a good idea wherever you trek: he can also explain and translate, if his language skills (and/or yours) are up to it, and he can also arrange for you to sleep overnight in villages. This is a great bonus and you get more trekking time the next day.

DO check carefully what's on offer with an organised trek: too many guides will just take you on a gentle stroll to a nearby hamlet where 20 other foreigners are already pestering people with their cameras. It is (still) so easy to get off the beaten track in Vietnam's hill country that it would be a shame to miss out on this unique and magic experience.

If you prefer to trek unaided and are fit and well equipped, get advice from a hotel (maps are very poor), tell them when (roughly) you plan to get back (calculate about 20 km a day outside the wet season) and go for it! Rural folk in Vietnam are usually gentle and incredibly hospitable.

DO pack good walking shoes if you plan to trek. Don't count on buying something when you get there, especially if you have big, Western feet. Something light but sturdy with a good tread is best, as you

will often be hiking down wet, muddy tracks or crossing paddy fields and streams. A lightweight waterproof is not a luxury, nor a sweater and some socks: even if you're sweltering down on the coast, it can be chilly in the highlands and freezing in the mountains.

Sensitive areas

Some sensitive areas in Vietnam, like military installations, prisons or nuclear research plants (there's at least one), are no different from restricted zones in any other country: if you try to enter or are found loitering, you will be stopped and questioned.

However, there are also areas that are sensitive because of political or ethnic dissent. The most notorious of these are in the Central Highlands, particularly near the borders with Cambodia and Laos. It is theoretically possible to go to many such places by requesting official permission. However, our advice (strictly unofficial, you understand) is, **DON'T** bother: it will be a lot of hassle, and they'll probably say no ('they' being the appropriate authorities). Just go: if you get stopped, it's not the end of the world (simply remember to carry your passport - and a photocopy of it, just in case). As a rule, you will find that the official line on things becomes progressively less strict, the further you get from the centres of power...

SWIMMING

Vietnam

Beaches

The topography of Vietnam means that it possesses an impressive coastline (some 3,200 km of it), with about 125 beaches of varying sizes and in varying stages of development. In fact, many beaches are still very unspoiled - or even completely wild, apart from local fishing activity. Urban Vietnamese are just beginning to adopt the beach holiday culture, but they mostly find time to go only in the blindingly hot summer months or on holiday weekends. If you also avoid the handful of seaside resorts

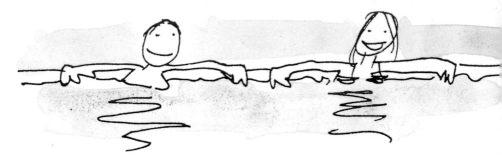

universally popular with this most gregarious of nations, you may have the beach practically to yourself.

If it's the local crowds you're looking for, then beaches as densely populated as the city centres at these times include:

Nearer Hanoi: Do Son south of Halong Bay, Som Son near Thanh Hoa and Cua Lo just outside Vinh.

Nearer Saigon: Vung Tau.

Between the two: Nha Trang and beaches near Danang.

During cooler seasons (when the sun is quite ferocious enough for frail, foreign skins), even these places will be quiet.

Beach destinations more adapted to foreign tastes include:

Nearer Hanoi: Nothing specific, but any pristine stretch of sand spotted while heading south along the coast, particularly just down the road from the hotspots mentioned above.

Nearer Saigon: Great beaches at Phan Thiet and Mui Ne, with thatched bungalows for rent right on the shore and luxury hotels nearby.

Between the two: Nha Trang deserves an honourable mention here, too, because despite rampant development, it has the best climate in Vietnam, a beautiful beach fringed with

coconut palms, a charming bay dotted with islands and several decent dive shops operating in town. No talk of beaches in Vietnam would be complete without mentioning China Beach *(Non nước)*, 15 km from Danang. A beautiful spot, swimming here can be dangerous at times, but when the wind is right, this is a surfer's paradise: an international surfing competition has been held here and the beach inspired Robert Duvall's notorious "Charlie don't surf" scene from the film Apocalypse Now.

DON'T go naked/topless on the beaches or in the water: culturally, this is a big no-no and would be asking for trouble.

DO protect yourself from the sun, even on apparently cloudy or hazy days: stories of foreigners with severe sunburn are too numerous to recount here.

DON'T camp on the beach: you might see local students doing it during their summer holidays, but foreigners are required to stay in hotels where they can be duly registered and accounted for.

Lakes and rivers

There are plenty of great places to swim inland, although many rivers are quite polluted by the time they've reached a decent size. Swimming in mountain streams can be very pleasant when the weather is warm. There are no dangerous parasites in still waters (watch out for leeches, though) and lakes and reservoirs abound.

Midnight dips

Midnight dips are fine, but remember that there's safety (and security) in numbers. Violent crime is still very rare in Vietnam, but **DON'T** tempt fate by leaving your stuff unattended on the beach!

AT A FRIEND'S
HOUSE

To be polite

DON'T drop by on a casual visit to friends in Vietnam without phoning or arranging it beforehand: you will embarrass them if their house is untidy, if they are busy, or if they simply don't have any food or drink to offer you.

DON'T be surprised if your friends have rather humble living quarters: even high-level people often live in quite modest circumstances.

DO greet older people present first. And don't forget to say goodbye to them before you leave.

What to bring

When you are invited by Vietnamese friends, you should arrive bearing some kind of gift. Popular favourites include a bag of fruit (a small selection of what's in season) or a bunch of flowers. However, as a rich foreign friend you could splash out on a bottle of wine or liquor, chocolates (if it's not too hot), or some sort of decorative trinket.

Before you make your purchase, **DO** check where the item comes from: the approval rating for locally made or Chinese items will be low; anything clearly imported from elsewhere will be better received. But **DON'T** expect to be thanked for your present or even to see it opened in front of you. It can be quite galling if you were hoping to share that nice bottle of champagne you brought along, but this is quite usual. You have been lucky enough to acquire merit by giving: what more do you want?!

What to leave outside

Your shoes: as in many Asian countries, people traditionally sit, rest and eat on the floor and the street is a dirty place, so the solution is to exchange your own footwear for some plastic sandals, flip-flops or slippers, offered by your host. This custom is a little less strictly applied in Vietnam than in certain countries (such as Thailand), but if you fall over a forest of footwear as you fight your way through your friend's door, **DON'T** believe him or her if s/he says politely that you can keep your clogs on: whip them off without more ado.

On the other hand, you can bring in just about anything else you want to - even your motorbike, if you have one and your friend doesn't have a courtyard or other secure parking place to leave it outside. Car owners sometimes even drive them into the ground floors of their houses for safekeeping.

When to say goodbye

You may still be having a good time when midnight strikes, but **DON'T** linger for too long: as a rule, such social occasions don't go on as long as they would do in your country. Leisure time is limited and people get up incredibly early in the morning.

DO be on the lookout for hints that the party's over... even if it's only nine in the evening. Everyone else has left? Your host looks at his watch and exclaims how late it is! Your host's spouse has already retired to bed. After a while, you might even be offered a not so subtle, but still Vietnamesely polite hint... "You go home now?"

When should you invite?

Vietnamese are expected to invite their family, friends or colleagues on a number of occasions, including:
- On their own birthday.
- After giving birth to a child.
- When they move to a new house or apartment.
- Upon starting a new job or getting a promotion.
- When they buy a big item like a new motorbike.

(In slang, it's called washing (or *rửa*) the new house, new motorbike or new-just-about-anything).

DO as they do. When it's your turn to invite, remember it's you who pays for everybody!

PAGODAS
& TEMPLES

Vietnam

No need to be shy

After reading guidebooks on other Asian countries like Thailand or China, travellers enter Vietnamese temples with apprehension. What should we do or not do? What are these customs about not touching the head of children and not pointing the feet?

Well, relax. You will find Vietnamese much more pragmatic and lenient in their daily life... including their conduct at temples and pagodas.

But first, a few obvious no-nos.

DON'T go to temples dressed as if you just walked off the beach. There is no special dress code other than to avoid obviously disrespectful attire: swimsuits, skimpy or torn T-shirts, head-turning shorts or low-cut blouses.

DON'T keep your shoes on if everyone else is taking them off. Rules vary from one temple to the next, just check for the presence of shoes and sandals on the front porch.

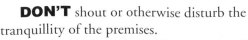

DON'T shout or otherwise disturb the tranquillity of the premises.

In traditional Buddhist temples, found mostly in Central and South Vietnam, there are a few additional etiquette rules.

DON'T touch monks if you are a woman - and the two classics: **DON'T** pat children's heads and **DON'T** point with your feet.

Apart from the above, you can just about be yourself... as long as you are a rather respectful self!

But the best rule of all remains: **DO** observe the locals to know what's OK and what's not.

Taking pictures

In most temples and pagodas you will be allowed (and sometimes even encouraged) to take pictures. However, in some Buddhist temples, taking pictures of certain Buddha statues is not allowed.

Asking before clicking is always respectful. No need to know the local language... simply show your camera and the object you would like to photograph.

Doing it the Vietnamese way

Trips to the countryside are always accompanied by a short visit to nearby temples.

Buy joss sticks, paper money or flowers at the entrance of the premises. Plant the lighted joss sticks in the vases placed for that purpose. Vietnamese like to disperse the sticks into as many vases as available... all deities should be thus

honoured. In front of any statue, preferably one of which you might know the background, hold your hands together at chest level and pray. Prayers are in the form of polite requests: for health, success, money, or whatever you need in your life at the present moment. Bow your head slightly and make space for the next visitor.

WEDDINGS
& FUNERALS

Tying the knot

If you spend some time in Vietnam, it probably won't be long before you are invited to a wedding. Although many weddings are less elaborate affairs than they used to be, there is still quite a procedure to be followed and it is widely respected.

Many marriages are more or less arranged by parents, but romantic love has definitely arrived in Vietnam with a vengeance. However, the first thing a prospective couple will do is compare horoscopes (and ages): any incompatibility here means all wedding bets are off.

If all is well, then the young things can get engaged. This is a separate ceremony, when the boy's relatives set off in procession to visit their future in-laws, bearing symbolic gifts in special red lacquered boxes. A fortune teller is consulted to set a date and time for the wedding. This may be as little as one month away or as much as three years later: it all depends on the stars and other factors, such as a period of mourning to be respected.

Even though the date may have been fixed far in advance, **DO** note that you will only receive your formal invitation about a week or ten days before the wedding. In fact, unless you are quite close to one or both of the couple, you may only be invited to the celebratory meal after the family ceremony, when the groom goes to his bride's family home to claim her.

DON'T count on seeing the formal signing of government marriage papers: this is done separately, either before or after the wedding - in fact, any time before the birth of a first child... although, according to the law, it should be the first step (see below).

When will the party start?

Owing to the complex superstitions determining auspicious moments for any two people to tie the knot, the date and time on your invitation may look like a printer's error, but,

DO be prepared for the party to be at seven o'clock on a

Sunday morning: this way you won't be too surprised, whenever it is...

DON'T turn up with a polite (to Western eyes) half-hour added to the time announced, or you may well miss the meal altogether - or find yourself celebrating the next wedding booked at the same restaurant! People are always busy in Vietnam and time is short, so the wedding feast may be over and the washing up done within an hour.

DON'T expect to party until dawn with close family and friends. No dancing or singing (except often deafening amplified music with a hired crooner). But at least there's always plenty to drink, even if you have to toast with total strangers. Vietnamese weddings are huge and formal affairs, with hundreds of colleagues and obligatory guests imposed by etiquette.

DON'T be surprised if you are shown wedding photos at the ceremony, already developed and arranged in albums: these are usually taken well before at a studio specialising in that sort of thing.

DON'T attempt to kiss the bride, Western style - unless of course she invites you to!

What about a present?

DO keep it simple: money is by far the easiest gift and is universally well received. One clean, nearly-new banknote of the largest local denomination should suffice, unless you are very close the one or both of the newly-weds and you want to give more, and/or **DO** buy something useful to help the happy couple set up their new home, as more and more newly-weds in Vietnam are now choosing to live by themselves, instead of with the groom's family as they did in the past.

Traditionally, the minimum acceptable money gift is one that covers the cost of the meal at the particular venue where the wedding takes place.

When choosing very upscale venues, couples run the risk of having friends or relatives politely declining the invitation or not showing up because they simply can't afford the cost.

Most people will identify themselves on the envelopes so the groom and bride will know the extent of their generosity and will have to match it when they themselves will be invited in that particular family.

Attending a funeral

If a friend or colleague invites you to a relative's funeral, it is really polite to show up, even if for a short time. Here's how you should go about it:

• On the way to the deceased's house (there are no funeral homes here), buy a funeral wreath at one of the specialised shops selling nothing but.

• At the friend's place, give the wreath then slowly walk around the wooden coffin, stopping a few seconds to look at the deceased's face. Coffins are sealed but there is a small windowpane placed above the deceased's head.

• Give proper condolences to your friend and mostly to the family's elders. If you don't know any Vietnamese words, just shake their hands and move on.

• You will most likely be invited to sit down and eat. It is polite to accept but don't linger at the table. Eat a few morsels then excuse yourself and leave.

Apart from funerals, you may be invited to commemorate someone's death anniversary. These anniversaries are celebrated much more scrupulously than birth anniversaries, especially when they involve a mother or father.

Some guidebooks actually say that it's polite to refuse. Not true. If you are extended a proper invitation - for instance with an actual date, time and place - then your hosts will be very honoured to have a foreigner at their gathering. Again, don't expect elaborate ceremonies, there will be none. Your presence and that of other guests are the most important elements of such celebrations. You will be introduced, asked to toast more than once, asked to eat more than you can probably ingest.

DON'T overindulge, even amidst the insistence of all family members: eat sparingly... the family might actually have to borrow money to feed all the guests.

DON'T linger around the table after the meal is over. They might expect other guests or may have other plans for the rest of the evening.

Although you probably will not have a chance to go to the cemetery where the deceased's body will be cremated or temporarily buried, and will also not be invited to the reinternment ceremony, you should be aware of a very particular funeral custom, mostly prevalent in the North.

The deceased are buried in a temporary location. Three years after, the remains are retrieved and the bones meticulously washed. What's left is then placed in a small coffin and taken to the final burial ground, most likely in the family's home village. Such burial grounds are scattered amongst the rice fields and can easily be seen from the road all over Vietnam's countryside. Usually a group of a dozen or so tombs, each of which is oriented in a different direction according to astrological considerations, regroup parents or souls from the same villages.

Your neighbour's funeral

You may know your neighbours or not but if one of them passes away, it won't go unnoticed.

The commotion caused by three days of preparation, feasting and endless queues of visitors will no doubt trouble your tranquillity. But it's the funerary music that will be the biggest challenge to your nerves and will test your degree of tolerance to local customs. Day and night, usually starting at six in the morning - weekends are not an excuse to start any later - the nasal sounds of the flutes and the banging of the tambourines will slowly drill their way into your brain, much like the famous Chinese water torture.

Unless you are specifically invited, you don't have to pay a visit or send flowers. You're only expected to tolerate the noise and activity.

Relax... Vietnamese, like all other human beings, only die once.

HOLIDAYS
& FESTIVALS

Vietnam

Têt, the biggest event of all

You can think of Têt as being the Vietnamese equivalent of Christmas, New Year and the annual holidays rolled into one.

• 'Christmas' as it's Vietnam's most important religious and family event.

• 'New Year' because it actually is the Lunar New Year.

• 'Annual holidays' since it is the only significant break from work for the majority of Vietnamese people.

DO take into account that although Vietnamese civil servants officially only get four days off, the whole country grinds to a halt one week before and up to two weeks after Têt. In the countryside, Têt is the occasion for a month long holiday, the only break most people will have in their working year.

DON'T plan any important meeting, business transaction or access to government services during that period.

DO note that flights into, out of, and inside the country will most probably be fully booked months in advance for the Têt period.

Têt (real name: *Têt Nhuyên Đán*) falls on the first day of the first lunar month and marks the advent of spring. In the solar calendar, it usually corresponds to late January or early February. It is a time of renewal and new beginnings, of family reunions and religious ceremonies. Beforehand, debts must be settled, arguments must be avoided, houses must be repaired, cleaned and decorated. The Vietnamese attach considerable importance to starting the year properly because it is believed that the first day will determine one's fortune for the rest of the year.

Among the many customs associated with Tết is the New Year's tree or *cây quất*. A few days before New Year, the streets will be filled with vendors offering this highly decorative mandarin tree, along with flowery branches of peach trees and other decorations. Markets and stores will be completely swamped with clients getting the last items for the preparation of lavish meals and receptions. Although the Government tries to keep prices from soaring during this important period, merchants do tend to make the most of the endless queues of clients.

Traditional meals - especially the *bánh chưng* - are an integral part of Tết festivities. Many different ceremonies are conducted at homes or at the pagodas to celebrate this important event.

Before midnight, the Spirit of the Hearth is sent to report on the family's doings during the year that is ending. Special care must be taken to try and have him depart in a positive frame of mind. Offerings and special prayers are addressed for deceased family members.

At midnight, in order to ward off evil spirits and welcome the good ones, great noises are made with firecrackers, drums and gongs. A few years ago, firecrackers were banned and replaced with fireworks at different parts of all major cities.

Vietnamese place extreme importance on the first visitor to pass the family door in the New Year.

DON'T visit any Vietnamese households on the morning of the first day of Têt unless you have been specifically instructed to do so. Vietnamese will go to considerable trouble to ensure that the first visitor to their home - and even to their office - is a 'proper' person, i.e. of the right zodiacal sign for the New Year and, if at all possible, a happy, lucky and wealthy person.

The lunar calendar

Each of the 12 lunar months has 29 or 30 days forming years with 355 days.

Approximately every third year, a thirteenth month is added (between the 3rd and 4th months) in order to keep the lunar calendar in synch with the solar year. Otherwise, the lunar 'seasons' would gradually fall back in the yearly cycle and would loose their link to the agricultural year.

The Vietnamese lunar calendar started in 2637 BC. In ancient cosmogony, Vietnamese used 60-year periods called *hồi,* divided in six 10-year periods (called *can* or 'heavenly stems') and five 12-year periods (called *giáp* or 'zodiacal stems'). The combination of a *can* and a *giáp* uniquely identified each year in a *hồi.*

You will no doubt discover your *giáp.* According to your year of birth you may be:

Rat	Dragon	Monkey
Buffalo	Snake	Chicken
Tiger	Horse	Dog
Cat	Goat	Pig

Hint: all Vietnamese calendars show both the solar and lunar dates. They are a must if you need to track down lunar dates.

A hundred anniversaries and festivals

Religious holidays

5th day of 3rd month

Remembering the Dead (*Thanh minh*). Families will visit the graves of deceased relatives and bring offerings of flowers, joss sticks, food and votive papers.

8th day of the 4th month

Buddha's Enlightenment. This is a day to visit pagodas. Especially in the South, many processions are organised for this occasion.

5th day of the 5th month

Summer Solstice. Offerings are made to spirits, ghosts and the God of Death.

15th day of the 7th month

Wandering Souls Day *(Tết Trung Nguyên)*. This is the second most important festival of the year. On this day, it is believed that the souls of the dead come back to the world of the living in order to have a taste of earthly pleasures. Ceremonial offerings are made for the souls of ancestors and the forgotten dead. Paper replicas of earthly objects are burnt and thus sent to the dead. It is also customary to release birds into the air and fish into water.

15th day of the 8th month

Originally the Mid-Autumn festival *(Tết Trung Thu)*, this event is now mostly celebrated by and for children. They gather in parks and on the streets dancing to the beat of drums while holding lanterns made of waxed paper surrounding a lit candle. Special stuffed glutinous rice cakes *(bánh dẻo)* and oven-baked cakes *(bánh nướng)* are prepared for this occasion.

28th day of the 9th month

Confucius's birthday.

25th day of the 12th month

Ông Táo, the Kitchen God, is believed to come and visit all households on this day. On this occasion, families buy a live fish, that they will later release into a lake or stream, burn paper money and address prayers that are to be relayed to *Ông trời* (Mr. Heaven) himself. The Kitchen God will rise back to Heaven on the fish, reporting the good and bad deeds of the households he visited as well as the prayers addressed to Heaven.

Christmas (based on solar calendar)

The Catholics and Protestants celebrate Christmas as in other countries with special masses and services. The commercial aspect of this event is starting to invade cities in both South and North Vietnam.

Secular holidays

February 3rd

Anniversary of the Founding of the Vietnamese Communist Party in 1930.

April 3rd

Liberation Day. The date on which Saigon surrendered to the North Vietnamese troops. Some cities also celebrate the date in March or April of 1975 when they were 'liberated' by the North Vietnamese Army.

May 1st

International Workers' Day.

May 19th

Ho Chi Minh's birthday.

September 2nd

This is both Vietnam's National Day and the anniversary of President Ho Chi Minh's death in 1969. The National Day commemorates the declaration of independence of the Democratic Republic of Vietnam by Ho Chi Minh in 1945.

Festivals

There are literally hundred of festivals held each year in cities and villages all over Vietnam. To name but a few:

First lunar month

4th - 5th   Traditional wrestling in Lieu Doi village (Ha Nam). This event also includes traditional poetry reciting and the preparation of regional culinary specialties.

5th   Horse-race in Quang Ngai province.

5th   Dong Da festival in Hanoi in memory of King Quang Trung who defeated the Chinese to liberate Thang Long citadel in 1789. A ceremony is held at the Khuong Thuong temple and prayers are conducted at the Dong Quan pagoda for the souls of the deceased.

6th   Catching the eel festival in Vinh Lac District (Vinh Phuc) is a celebration to wish for plentiful harvests and prosperous lives.

8th - 10th   Spring market for handicraft products and ornamental plants in Van Ban District (Nam Dinh).

10th   Martial arts competition in Huong Phu District (Thua Thien Hue). Hundreds of young girls and boys participate in competitions where all schools of martial arts in Vietnam are represented.

13th   Lim Folk Song festival in Bac Ninh Province.

Second lunar month

15th   Perfume Pagoda Pilgrimage in Ha Tay. This festival, the longest in Vietnam, lasts for nearly two months (from the 6th day of the first lunar month to the end of the third moon) with the 15th as the main festival day. Hundreds of thousands of pilgrims visit the numerous pagodas and grottos dispersed on the mountainsides, while admiring the scenery. If you are not a crowd seeker, it probably is best to visit Perfume Pagoda outside the festival period.

spring   Sometime in the 2nd lunar month, an elephant race in organised in Buon Don (Dak Lak). This highly colourful event stages a 2 km race where 10 elephants compete to the sounds of drums and gongs.

Third lunar month

10th   The Hung Kings festival in Phu Tho is a sacred event for Vietnamese. Many Hanoians and Northerners will use this opportunity to visit their land of origin. Activities include folk song singing and drum beating contests as well as other games.

9th - 11th   Truong Yen festival in Hoa Lu District (Ninh Binh) commemorates a national hero, King Dinh Tien Hoang, credited with unifying the country after repressing the Rebellion of Vassals. It involves a mock battle against the Chinese invaders.

15th   The Do Temple festival in Tu Son district (Bac Ninh) honours the memory of the eight kings from the Ly dynasty. Processions, cock fighting, traditional wrestling and human pawn chess games.

20th - 23rd   Thap Ba festival at the towers of Po Nagar north of Nha Trang. The largest event in the region, this festival honours Po Nagar, Mother-goddess and founder of the country, who taught the people the secrets of rice cultivation.

Fourth lunar month

1st   Traditional silver carving village Dong Xam festival in Thai Binh province. The boat races and traditional opera representations (*cheo* and *ca tru*) attract a large crowd of spectators.

8th   Dau Pagoda festival in Thuan Thanh district (Bac

Ninh province). This event, in honour of Mrs Man Muong who is credited with successfully fighting off drought, involves a procession and folk games.

9th Giong festival in Phu Dong village, Gia Lam district (Hanoi) in memory of the mythical hero who defeated the An invaders. This festival stages cultural shows, including water puppets.

23rd - 27th Chua Xu festival, the largest in the Mekong Delta, is held on mount Sam in Chau Doc (An Giang). Visitors and pilgrims come to ask for happiness and prosperity as well as to participate in the cultural events.

Fifth lunar month

5th Water festival in Nha Trang where city dwellers flock to the beach to bathe while getting rid of parasites and worms.

Sixth lunar month

16th Greeting the Whale festival in Tien Giang province.

Seventh lunar month

30th Lang Ong festival in Ho Chi Minh City on the occasion of the anniversary of the death of Le Van Duyet, officer in the Nguyen dynasty and governor of Gia Dinh province.

Eighth lunar month

9th Buffalo Fighting festival in Do Son (Hai Phong). Winners and losers will be sacrificed to the water genie who saved the population from natural calamities. The meat will be distributed to the spectators as a sign of sharing happiness.

Ninth lunar month

13th Keo Pagoda festival (Thai Binh Province) in honour of a Buddhist monk who cured Emperor Ly Than Tong of a fatal disease. This festival comprises

Buddhist ceremonies as well as games and folk performances.

15th - 20th   Co Le Pagoda festival in Nam Dinh Province in honour of another Buddhist monk, sorcerer Nguyen Minh Khong, one of the originators of bronze casting.

Tenth lunar month

15th   Moon festival (*ook-om-bok*) in Southwest Vietnam by the Khmer people. To thank the Moon for the good harvest and the plentiful fish catch, offerings of glutinous rice, bananas, coconuts and manioc are brought out as the moon rises over the horizon. The next day, colourful boat races are organised on the river for the hundreds of thousands of spectators that flock to the river's edge.

18th - 19th   Nguyen Trung Truc Temple festival (An Giang province) in memory of this commander of the revolt against the French. It involves ceremonies, exciting games and a re-enactment of the battle against a French ship.

Eleventh lunar month

11th   An Lu Temple festival in Hai Phong in memory of Tran Hung Dao, a national hero who defeated the Mongolians

18th   Trung Do festival in Ha Tay in memory of King Ly Nam De.

22nd   Dong Quan festival at Chan Tien pagoda, Hanoi.

Twelfth lunar month

15th   Ca Ong festival in Khanh Hoa.

23rd   Thai Duong festival in Thua Thien Hue to worship the genie Thai Duong.

And on the 30th day of the last lunar month, rice cooking contest in Tu Trong village (Thanh Hoa).

LANGUAGE
& CULTURE

Vietnamese language survival kit

Note: this section is not intended to replace a phrasebook. You can buy those from any postcard seller on just about any street corner in Vietnam. It will, however, present you with useful language tips that you won't find in standard phrasebooks.

Why bother learning Vietnamese?

Let's say things as they are, learning the Vietnamese language, unless you're Chinese, is no easy task. Why bother then? Because:

• It is a challenge...! Well, if you didn't like challenges, you probably wouldn't be running around in strange countries in the first place.

• It is the best window into Vietnamese culture. Learning even the basics will help you understand the country and its people.

• It is a very good icebreaker and will help you enter in contact with people at the market, on the street, in the villages.

• Vietnamese are extremely rewarding towards those who make the effort of learning their language. Expect more smiles, even friendlier rapports and lower prices when you try and utter the local lingo.

• And to top it off, Vietnamese language also has its easy sides. Yes, really. Like a totally phonetic spelling system, and an extremely easy grammar with no verb tenses, declinations, word gender or even plural forms.

Why can't they understand me?

One of the most irritating hurdles on the rocky road to learning Vietnamese, is the seeming inability of Vietnamese to understand what we perceive as rather good renditions of Vietnamese words and sentences. After several unsuccessful tries, if you're lucky, a Vietnamese among the crowd that will have gathered to 'help', will catch the phrase you are desperately trying to get across and repeat it to the audience who will then oh! and ah! at leisure. And you will be left fuming... "But that's exactly what I have been repeating for the last five minutes" you will be thinking.

DO know that Vietnamese will not easily understand foreigners' accents. Contrary to English speakers, Vietnamese are not used to their language being twisted in unusual dialects and strange accents. They also have had very little previous contact with Vietnamese-speaking foreigners.

DO understand that tones are as important as consonants and syllables and Vietnamese have a hard time guessing tones or even making the link between two words with the same spelling, but with different tones.

DON'T get shy... get out there and talk. Expect a few laughs, a few blind stares, but also a lot of encouragement.

DON'T expect too much technical help from your friends in your quest to learn the language. Not because they don't want to or shy away from the effort, but understanding the technicalities and difficulties of one's own language doesn't come with the language itself. That's why there are teachers!

DO remember, if you're serious about learning the language, there are classes... available whenever you are.

Nobody is really tone-deaf

"I can't learn Vietnamese, I'm tone-deaf."
This is probably the most common excuse you will hear. Interestingly enough, it's not the inability to hear other people's tones that's at stake here, but rather to hear and control one's own voice.

Every language - apart from some computer generated voice messages - uses inflexions and intonations. Any Westerner will recognise the difference between identical sentences where the meaning is changed by tones, such as: "This is my dog" or "This is my dog?".

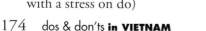

A really tone deaf person would have a hard time understanding English... or any other language for that matter.

DO try and recognise the tones and inflections that you use in your own speech. You will have to learn to control them.

Try the following exercise, saying 'I do' using intonation to signify different meanings.

- I do? (surprise and interrogation rendered by a rising tone on do)
- I do! (determination rendered by mid-tones with a stress on do)

- I do! (you are differentiating yourself from other people rendered by a high tone on a stressed I)
- I do. (imitating a toneless and unstressed computer generated voice as rendered by many robot characters in films)
So you're really tone-deaf? Better take care at the altar... you could be saying I do? instead of I do!

One of the most difficult situations to master is to control one's rising tone tendencies. In most Western languages, rising tones are used profusely in a variety of contexts: to indicate questions, disbelief, insistence, to ask for confirmation or simply as part of a normal sentence pattern (ever noticed how Irishmen use rising tones?).

In Vietnamese, as the tone alters the meaning of the word, a Western-style rising tone question will - unless the final Vietnamese syllable happens to have a rising tone - baffle your interlocutor. No wonder he won't be able to answer your question...

Examples:

1- The question trap.

I want to ask "This is my house?" *(đây là nhà tôi)*, so my voice goes up on 'house'.

The sentence then becomes: "This is a gloomy house" *(đây là nhà tối)*. Slightly confusing...

2- The exclamation trap.

I want to say to the new parents "Wow, your son looks like his father". Because I tend to raise the pitch of the last word, 'father' becomes 'piss-pot'. Slightly embarrassing...

3- The progression trap.

The first time, you pronounced the word at your normal voice pitch. But being asked to repeat the sentence, you add a rising tone indicating something like "Wasn't that the right word?" and change the meaning altogether. More incomprehension and growing irritation leads you to repeat the phrase louder and more assertively with a different tone ending - possibly an assertive down tone this time. Your interlocutor is confronted with a still wider choice of words...

Why is Vietnamese written in Roman characters?

Ever heard of Alexandre de Rhodes? Probably not, but this priest is credited to have developed and spread the use of the current Vietnamese alphabet in replacement of a special Chinese script that the Vietnamese were using before.

A very, very long time ago...(before the 13th century)

Vietnamese was written using the standard Chinese characters (*chữ nho*).

A very long time ago... (from the 13th to the 17th century)

The Vietnamese decided to adapt the classical Chinese characters to their spoken language and devised their own writing using mostly the phonetic significance of the Chinese characters (instead of their actual meaning). This was called *chữ Nôm* and was used in parallel with the more classical system.

A long time ago... in 1627

Alexandre De Rhodes, a brilliant French Jesuit scholar, designed a radically different writing system in order to help mostly illiterate peasants read the Bible. The system was a phonetic transliteration of spoken Vietnamese using Roman characters to which were added tone markers and a few other diacritical marks.

The system, called *chữ quốc ngữ,* became so popular among the people that it rapidly displaced the Chinese script that only the mandarin and higher officials could decipher.

Nowadays

The language has evolved slightly but, by and large, the phonetic basis of the writing system has been maintained. So take heed, spoken Vietnamese might be difficult to master, but reading and writing it is easier than most other Asian languages.

YES OR NO?

What does yes really mean?

We did mention that Vietnamese liked to say 'yes' way more often than 'no'. There is one word for no and that's *'không'*, but for yes... the nuances are nearly infinite.

There are the *'dạ'* and *'ừ'* used mostly at the end of the other interlocutors sentences and having more the meaning of 'I've heard you' or 'keep going' than a solid 'yes'. *'Vâng'* is a more general - but sometimes very vague - yes; literally, it means 'you are right'.

Most of the times, the Vietnamese will use the verb contained in the question to express a 'yes-approval'. Something like:

Q. Did you see the football match yesterday?
A. I saw.
Q. Do you have a motorbike?
A. I have.

Watch out for negative questions! Vietnamese say yes to approve the negation.

Q. This isn't your house, is it?
A. Yes. (meaning: yes, it's **not** my house)

Double negative questions? Forget those, you'd be lucky if any Vietnamese would understand such a convoluted sentence and even luckier to guess correctly what a yes would mean.

Unfortunately, knowing how to say yes is the easy part. Understanding what a Vietnamese really means when he answers yes takes a few years of practice and experience.

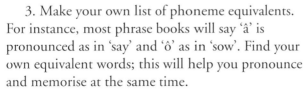

Beware of the Vietnamese yes

- Ask all questions several times over and in different ways.
- Never give the answer in a question. Ask open questions, not leading questions.
- **DON'T** ask negative questions.
- Avoid 'either or' questions.

Ten tips to learning the lingo

1. You have to learn to hear your own voice! Tape yourself... listen - not to the words - but to your intonations and inflexions. Ask someone who has good imitation skills (what we usually refer to as 'a good ear') or who knows a bit of Vietnamese to help you decode your own voice.

2. **DON'T** skip the basics: pronunciation. Vietnamese phonemes are quite different and learning the alphabet is a worthwhile endeavour.

3. Make your own list of phoneme equivalents. For instance, most phrase books will say 'â' is pronounced as in 'say' and 'ô' as in 'sow'. Find your own equivalent words; this will help you pronounce and memorise at the same time.

4. Revisit the basics often. Can you tell - and pronounce - the difference between *'quen'* and *'quên'* or *'tây'*, *'tâi'*, *'tay'* and *'tai'*...? Pronunciation and tones are two different but equally difficult

challenges of the language.

5. At first, exaggerate the tones and even use your hands to mime them.

6. Speak loudly and listen to yourself. After having said a sentence, try and rehear it mentally to see where you have placed the tones and inflexions.

7. Learn a few introductory sentences and use them over and over again, slowly building from there to enlarge your repertoire.

8. When a Vietnamese is correcting you on a word, make sure you know if he is correcting your pronunciation or your tone. Again, use your hands for tones.

9. Look at the shop signs and advertisements. The Vietnamese phonetic alphabet makes it easy (!) to practise saying the words even if - at first - you don't understand their meaning. These signs are like an open-air dictionary, albeit with limited vocabulary.

10. There are no short cuts. If you really want to learn, you'll have to make the effort. Get books, buy tapes, and practice.

USEFUL
VIETNAMESE
PHRASES

XANH

Introduction

It's the most convenient way to start learning and also the answer to the most common opening questions from Vietnamese.

My name is ...	*Tên tôi là ...*
I come from...	*Tôi là người ...*
I am married	*Tôi có vợ* (I have a wife)
	Tôi có chồng (I have a husband)
I am single	*Tôi chưa cô vợ / chồng*
	(I don't have a wife / husband yet)
I have ... children	*Tôi có ... con*
I don't have any children yet.	*Tôi chưa có con*

In the above example we have used *'Tôi'* to say I. Although correct, this form of 'I' is used only sparingly when one doesn't know the interlocutor well and wants to keep a certain distance. In all other cases... read on.

The family tree

It does get tricky rather quickly, even for such simple words as 'me' and 'you'.

The family model has permeated even the language itself. In Vietnamese, people refer to themselves and to others with words taken from the family analogy: older sister, younger brother, grandfather, maternal uncle... The trick is to guess (or better, to ask) the age of your interlocutor in order to adjust the 'you and I' accordingly. But the nuances are nearly infinite and mastering a dozen versions of 'I' in normal speech does not come easily.

This is where you will need the family tree. Simply (!) project yourself and your interlocutor in a hypothetical family and use the appropriate, 'you' and 'I' pronouns.

For instance:

(a) You are in your early twenties and meet a woman in her forties. On a first meeting, you would call her *chị* and would use *em* as 'I'.

(b) You meet a man in his mid-fifties. On a first meeting, especially in a formal occasion (business, official introduction), you would address him as *ông* and refer to yourself as *tôi*. Later, should you become much closer to him and his family, you might have to switch to a more personal and appropriate relationship, calling him *tôi* depending on the age of your own father and refer to yourself as *bác* or *chú*.

The Family Vocabulary

	'You'	'I'
Great-grandparent (male/female)	*cụ ông /* *cụ bà*	*cháu* or *chát*
Grandfather	*ông*	*cháu*
Grandmother	*bà*	*cháu*
Father	*bố*	*con*
Mother	*mẹ*	*con*
Paternal uncle (older/younger than your father)	*bác / chú*	*cháu*
Maternal uncle (older/younger than your mother)	*bác / cậu*	*cháu*
Paternal aunt (older/younger than your father)	*bác / cô*	*cháu*
Maternal aunt (older/younger than your mother)	*bác / dì*	*cháu*
Older brother	*anh*	*em*
Older sister	*chị*	*em*
Younger brother or sister	*em*	*anh / chị*
Nephew or niece	*cháu*	*bác / chú / cậu / dì*
Cousin (older M / older F / younger M or F)	*anh họ / chị họ / em họ*	*anh / chị / em*
Friends	*bạn*	*tôi*
Teacher (male)	*thầy*	*em*
Teacher (female) and young women	*cô*	*em*
Children	*cháu*	*bác / chú / cậu / dì*

As an outsider, you can simplify things...
• Instead of using '*chào anh*', '*chào em*' and all the other proper forms of address, you can use the more general '*xin chào*' which

doesn't necessitate any of the family pronouns.

• As a general all-purpose 'I', you can use your own name. Mostly artists and VIPs do this, but your foreigner status will allow it without a problem... if you can get used to it.

• Start with the basics: with children, use *cháu*, with younger people, it's *em* for both men and women, with people older than you or that you don't know well, use *anh* for men and *chị* for women. Try and remember to use *ông* (men) and *bà* (women) for the elderly. Use *tôi* or your own surname as 'I'.

Although sometimes, it gets more complicated...

For instance, when you start seriously dating a Vietnamese man or woman, after being presented to the family, you should address each member from the standpoint of your partner in his/her family. That means you might have to refer to yourself as "younger brother" even if you are older... But we're not there yet, right?

Diffusing situations

After having introduced yourself, you're definitely going to need some phrases for tricky situations to at least appear unruffled, even if you're feeling the opposite. This way you won't embarrass any Vietnamese by yourself losing face and thus making them feel bad for you!

Không sao đâu (often shortened to *không sao*) - is the king of them all, and translates roughly as 'never mind', 'no problem' or 'don't worry'. Will be invaluable in countless situations.

Vô tư đi! - is an invitation to 'take it easy', 'slow down' and just generally chill out.

Quên đi!- 'forget it', 'let it drop', useful for defusing and cutting short a difference of opinion. *Thôi!* meaning 'cease', is a milder way of ending a conversation that is getting out of hand.

Asking for help

You will notice that most Vietnamese, among themselves, when dealing with officials, sales clerks, or colleagues always place themselves in the position of 'asking for help'. This seems to be the polite and usual way of 'getting things done' in this country.

Excuse me...	*xin lỗi...*
(Please) help me...	*giúp tôi...*
Please give me...	*xin cho tôi...*
I need...	*tôi cần...*
I ask your permission to...	*tôi xin phép...*

Asking directions

The tricky part here is to get them to understand your question but never give them a chance to simply answer by 'yes'. A question like 'Is this (pointing) the way to the Opera House?' will lead you nowhere as a 'yes' will mean either 'yes', 'no', 'I don't know', 'I have no clue what you're talking about' or 'I don't want to talk with foreigners'...

Where is ... street?	*Phố ... ở đâu?*
Excuse me, where are the washrooms?	*Xin lỗi, vệ sinh ở đâu?*
I need a taxi/mototaxi/cyclo.	*Tôi cần một xe tắc xi / một xe ôm / một xi-clô*

The '*đi*' family

The *đi* family is an endless one (*đi* on its own means 'go'), since when tacked on to something else, it becomes an invitation or an imperative, giving possibilities such as:

Vào đi!	- (please) come in	*Ngồi đi!*	- (please) sit down
ăn đi!	- (please) eat	*Uống đi!*	- (please) drink
Im đi!	- shut up!	*Đi đi!*	- go away!
... and so on.			

Too much!

Another important family to meet is the *quá* clan. *Quá* refers to anything that is too much, too many, excessive, or overflowing.

Đắt quá! - that's too expensive! Learn this one right away: Vietnamese people will start any bargaining or negotiating like this without hesitation or any prior knowledge of the true value of a product: the first price you hear (except maybe for a postage stamp) is automatically too high, and should be taken as a starting-point, a challenge, an insult, a joke - as anything you like except the actual price to be paid.

Mệt quá!   - I'm very tired
Tiếc quá!   - what a pity, what a shame
Đẹp quá!   - how pretty/handsome you are!
Quá khen! - you're too kind! (ie, flattery will get you nowhere...)

Make them laugh and you'll win their hearts!

Vietnamese like to smile and laugh in all situations. A little bit of humour will go a long way. But sometimes you will have them laughing at you without knowing why.

Vietnamese language is monosyllabic and tonal, making it ideal for puns, plays on words and... hilarious mistakes by foreigners who are giving it a try.

To understand the most common Vietnamese jokes, one must know the following basic analogies:

The birds and the butterflies!

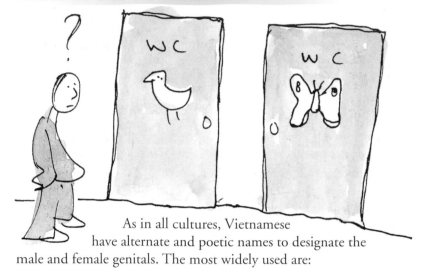

As in all cultures, Vietnamese have alternate and poetic names to designate the male and female genitals. The most widely used are:

Chim, meaning 'bird' for the penis,
Bướm, meaning 'butterfly' for the vulva.
So anytime you talk about birds or butterflies, expect giggles and innuendoes.

Rice or noodles?

Do you prefer rice or noodles? Sometimes the question is legitimate, like when you are sitting in a restaurant ready to order. But most of the time, it's just another Vietnamese running gag.

Cơm, is 'rice', as you will no doubt learn very quickly. But it is also used to refer to your wife (or regular partner in Western cultures).

Phở, is the famous Vietnamese 'noodle soup', but in this context, when opposed to rice, it usually refers to a lover (or mistress).

Of course, any stated preference will be interpreted as 'wife' or 'lover' and will get your Vietnamese friends laughing. After they recover from their hysteria, they will usually try and explain the inside joke and will conclude with the common Vietnamese answer for married men. Literally translated, it goes something like:

'In the morning I take my wife (rice) to eat noodles. At noon, I take my lover (noodles) to eat rice. At night, rice and noodles go back to their respective houses.'

Colour blind?

Mild colour blindness is characterised by the inability to distinguish between greens from blues. Does this have anything to do with the peculiar fact that, in Vietnamese, there is only one word to refer to both green and blue? One must use periphrases *'xanh lá cây'* (plant leaf green/blue) for green and *'xanh da trời'* (sky green/blue) for blue. Were Vietnam's forefathers more prone to colour blindness?

Student talk

With so many students, from kindergarten to university level, rushing to learn English, there's bound to be some mutual influence between the two languages. Apart from a flurry of new words picked up by the Vietnamese to adjust the language to modernity, a more curious trend is 'student talk'.

It goes like this: you take a common Vietnamese expression and you translate each word in English using, when possible, an alternate but correct meaning. You then constitute a baffling expression.

For instance the expression *'không sao đâu'* means something like 'nothing to it', but *không* is no, one of the many meanings of *sao* is 'star' and *đâu* can mean, among other things, 'where'. Putting it all together you get: 'No star where!' which can now be used as a way of saying 'there's nothing to it!'.

DO try to talk with students. They are Vietnam's future and you will learn a great deal from them. It's actually very easy, as most are keen to meet foreigners and practice their English. Just hang around in parks and public places and strike up a conversation as you see them walking by. They'll love it.

The North and the South

Each region in Vietnam has its own accent, sometimes so different that even Vietnamese must learn to adjust. However, the two main streams of Vietnamese language are characterised as 'Northern' or 'Southern'.

The main differences are:
• Tones: six in the North, five in the South.
• Accent: much more staccato in the North and more singsong in the South.
• Pronunciation: the letters 'd' and 'r' and 'gi' are pronounced 'z' in the North and 'y' in the South. For example: the Vietnamese national costume, the *áo dài,* is pronounced *'ao zai'* in the North and *'ao yai'* in the South.
• There are many differences in vocabulary:

Some North-South differences

English	Hanoi	Ho Chi Minh City
father	*bố*	*ba*
mother	*mẹ*	*má*
a little	*một ìt*	*chút xìu*
expensive	*đắt*	*mắc*
fast	*nhanh*	*lẹ*
fat	*béo*	*mập*
ill	*ốm*	*bệnh*
no problem	*không có gì*	*không có chi*
what	*gì*	*chi*
yes	*vâng*	*dạ* (pronounced 'ya')
airport	*sân bay*	*phi trường*
blanket	*chăn*	*mền*
boat	*thuyền*	*ghe*
bowl	*bát*	*chén*

box of matches	bao diêm	hộp quẹt
bus	xe buýt	xe đò
car	ô tô	xe hơi
envelope	phong bì	phong thơ
floor	tầng	lầu
fridge	tủ lạnh	máy lạnh
kilogram	cân	ký
letter	thư	thơ
mosquito net	màn	mùng
motorbike	xe máy	xe gắn máy
office	cơ quan	công sở, sở
right hand	tay phải	tay mặt
road	đường	lộ
shop	hiệu	tiệm
soap	xà phòng	xà bông
thousand	nghìn	ngàn
traffic jam	tắc đường	kẹt xe
umbrella	cái ô	cây dù
USD	đô la Mỹ	Mỹ kim
call	gọi	thắng
come in	vào	vô
cut hair	cắt tóc	hớt tóc
hurry up	nhanh lện	lẹ lên
joke	đùa, nói đùa	dỡn, nói dỡn
lie	nói dối	nói sạo
love	yêu	thương
take pictures	chụp ảnh	chụp hình
turn right	rẽ tay phải	quẹo tay mặt
turn	rẽ	quẹo
cauliflower	hoa lơ	cải bông
	(The French word súp lơ is also used)	
chicken egg	trứng gà	hột gà
corn, maize	ngô	bắp

custard apple	*na*	*mãng cầu*
fruit	*quả*	*trái*
fry	*rán*	*chiên*
glass	*cốc*	*ly*
peanut	*lạc*	*đậu phụng*
pineapple	*quả dứa*	*trái thơm*
pork	*thịt lợn*	*thịt heo*
restaurant	*hiệu ăn*	*tiệm ăn*
spring roll	*nem*	*chả giò*
tea	*chè*	*trà*

Other expressions

Comrade *(đồng chí)* is still used sparingly in the North as a means of addressing people. You will hear it mostly at the market. Southerners will smile if you use it there...

Southerners are more inclined to forego the strict family nomenclature and use *tôi* (I) and *bạn* (friend) more frequently.

DON'T be put off by the different accents. Northern Vietnamese is considered as the official one and will be understood by all... once you master it. If you happen to start learning in Ho Chi Minh City, that should not be a problem either as the national television features presenters using either accents so most people will understand a Southerner... and maybe even a foreigner with a Southern accent!